BENEATH TROUBLED SKIES

Poems of Scotland at War, 1914–1918

BENEATH TROUBLED SKIES

Poems of Scotland at War, 1914–1918

foreword by
Hew Strachan

commentaries by
Yvonne McEwen

compiled and edited by
Lizzie MacGregor

Scottish **Poetry** Library

Polygon

First published in 2015 by
The Scottish Poetry Library
5 Crichton's Close
Edinburgh, EH8 8DT

and

Polygon,
an imprint of Birlinn Ltd
West Newington House, 10 Newington Road
Edinburgh, EH9 1QS

www.scottishpoetrylibrary.org.uk
www.polygonbooks.co.uk

ISBN 978 1 84697 3321

Typeset by Edward Crossan in Verdigris MVB

Printed and bound by
TJ International, Padstow, Cornwall

The publishers acknowledge investment from Creative Scotland and
are grateful for the support of the Scottish Government in publishing
this collection.

Contents

Foreword

The relationship between the First World War and poetry is a symbiotic one. Many, especially those whose language is English, confront the war for the first time through its poets, but that 'strange meeting' may also be the reader's first encounter with poetry. Much of the subject matter of war – on existence at the borders between life and death, on coping with loss, and on finding meaning in suffering – inherently lends itself to poetry.

These attributes are not of course unique to the First World War. All war has the capacity to raise questions about its utility and moral purpose, but for Britain the First World War is definitive in this respect. It was fought by a literate generation, the beneficiary of compulsory primary education, which was used to seeing verse (even if much of it was doggerel) printed in daily newspapers. Moreover, poetry – as the chronological structure of this book testifies – carried an immediacy in conveying war's emotional charge that was denied to prose. It lived in the present and so was relieved of hindsight. The great memoirs of 1914–18 – even those written by men who were themselves poets, such as Siegfried Sassoon or Edmund Blunden – were by and large completed after the war, most of them a decade later, and so they refined, distilled and ordered personal experiences into some sort of coherent narrative. The poems in this volume portray lived events in the order in which they occurred, going forwards not backwards, in anticipation more than subsequent reflection. Outcomes could be uncertain when they were written, and the poets themselves did not yet know how the war would end, or whether they themselves would live to see it. Several did not. Their poems could not – by definition – be tainted by distance or certainty.

That said, it is remarkable how consistently the same themes recur. Appeals in 1914 to Scotland's military past and to Scots to join Scottish regiments, by A. Stodart Walker and J. B. Symons, mirror the more jingoistic and forgettable effusions published by the press, but even in the opening year of the war the mood of many, including Charles Hamilton Sorley, perhaps Scotland's greatest war poet, might have been more reflective and nuanced. Nonetheless, what remains striking is that few north of the border seem to have captured, as fully as Rupert Brooke did, the dilemma posed by the war: the challenge of simultaneously accepting the war's necessity and being frank about the personal fears generated by its outbreak. Brooke's wartime status as *the* English-language poet of the war – now of course forfeited to Wilfred Owen – rested on his capacity to embrace both the obligation of war and its potential for loss of life and even of meaning. This ambivalence in Brooke is often overlooked and in this book is perhaps most coherently expressed in E. A. Mackintosh's 'War, The Liberator'. Mackintosh's poem demands that the 'authoress' of 'Non-Combatants', to which it is a riposte, acknowledge the 'fragments of high Romance' in war. Mackintosh accepts death but refuses to become its slave. His voice is an authentic one, a strong presence in the book; what is remarkable about this particular poem is that it was written not in 1914, but in 1917, shortly before its author was himself killed.

Mackintosh was unusual among Scottish poets. For most of them war rarely has a redeeming purpose. That of course is not unusual in the poetry of the First World War, much of it overwhelmed by death and disfigurement, by grief and loss. If disillusionment arose from the belief that the war had no utility, then that is the dominant theme of this collection. And yet that does not make the poems unpatriotic. Throughout this volume there is a strong sense of Scotland's identity. The grief is not just personal, it is also public – a sense of the collective loss inflicted on the community by war. It is nonetheless a community that for the most part looks inwards, whose members know each other, at least subliminally. After the war many poets and writers, Siegfried Sassoon and Erich Maria Remarque among them, reflected on their inability to reintegrate with the homes they had left. They had been changed by the war, and the war too had transformed and even revolutionised their parent societies. In the late 1920s they turned to the familiarity of the military world, its comradeship and shared experiences. While the war went on, however, as the historians of several nations have now demonstrated, many citizen soldiers were sustained by an idealised vision of what they had left behind. Wartime patriotism has been redefined in the process: not so much flag waving and more home and hearth. Today's scholarship also sees it as nostalgic and backward-looking. And so are the poems published here. Apart from Jean Guthrie-Smith's description of the canteen in a national shell-filling factory, the Scotland of these poets is overwhelmingly agricultural and rural, a Scotland of mountain and moor, not of munitions production and shipbuilding.

So this is a book shaped by the soldier's war. In 1914 Scotland produced proportionately more volunteers for Kitchener's New Armies than the rest of Britain and, although in absolute terms the big cities provided more recruits than did smaller rural communities, the latter made a greater relative contribution given their size. The jobs from which the soldiers in these poems have been torn are those of shepherding and ploughing, not welding and riveting. The regret is that their passing will leave land untilled, and so agricultural – not industrial – output will fall. And yet the latter defined Scotland's greatest contribution to Britain's war effort: Glasgow, 'the second city of the empire', supplied an imperial fighting machine and many of its allies. It also became the principal home of socialism, radicalism and pacifism. 'Red Clydeside' is almost invisible in Scottish poetry of the period. Glasgow's opposition to the war was paradoxical on two counts: first because the war meant the city prospered, and second because its industrial strength increasingly protected its men from the dangers of military service. The introduction of conscription in 1916 caused a slump in Scottish recruiting precisely because so many Scots were in reserved occupations vital to the production of goods necessary for the war effort.

The poems evoke an 'old' Scotland in another sense too. Women's experience of the war is refracted less through their contribution to the war effort (although Jean Guthrie-Smith is an exception here) and more through their definition of themselves in relation to their menfolk. Their voices are among the most strident when confronting the loss of men in battle; their role in war is therefore that of self-denial and sacrifice. Very often they render their greatest service to the war by giving their men, whether as mothers or lovers. May Wedderburn Cannan made a contribution to the war effort by working in an office. But her poem, 'To a Clerk, Now at the Wars', does not trumpet her work; instead it envies the male clerk whom she has replaced because he is now freed to take an active part in the fighting. The woman's part is treated as inherently secondary precisely because it is not located in the front line.

The comparisons here are with English poetry, the best of which has now formed a canon; few Scots poets have gained admission. Does this in itself suggest that the Scottish experience of the war has a distinctly Scottish voice, but one that speaks only to Scots? There are writers in this book who in prose had an impact across the empire and even in the United States, most obviously John Buchan, the creator of Richard Hannay, and Ian Hay, whose novel *The First Hundred Thousand* captured the voices of Kitchener's New Armies through the medium of a Scottish battalion. The early poems of the war urge Scots to show the rest of Britain what Scotland can do; they tell Scots to vie with the other nations of the United Kingdom, and do so in the certainty that, while its components possess separate identities, they are also defined by a common one, that of Britain and its empire. Some of the most directly effective poems are written by officers of Scottish background but English education, including Charles Hamilton Sorley and E. A. Mackintosh. Both Robert Service and John Buchan used a more vernacular tongue, but were also products of empire, and they looked out from Scotland as well as in. Poems in Scots and in Gaelic self-evidently make clear a distinct cultural as well as national identity. It may be surprising that it is not one shaped by religion (the Kirk is entirely absent from this collection), but across Europe the war seems to have done more to promote the loss of faith than to affirm it. Nor in most cases is it a political nationalism. But it bears testimony to the war's role in creating a sense of national difference, in relation both to the lands in which Scots served and to the other nations of Britain. By 1918 Scotland did not stand where it had stood in 1914 – either in its sense of itself or in its relationship to others. There is therefore a difference between poems about the war which happen to be about Scots, and poems which are more directly addressed to Scotland itself. One consequence of the war was that its experience made that distinction increasingly significant: Scots took up arms for Britain and the empire, but Scotland became more conscious of itself as it fought.

The poet who embodied that response in the later twentieth century was Hugh MacDiarmid (or Christopher Murray Grieve), a veteran of the campaign in Macedonia for whom the war provoked political as well as cultural nationalism. Most of those included in this fresh and original collection are less well-known than he. But Sorley and Mackintosh can stand with the best of the English-language canon, and both died too soon in the war to have reached the maturity of which they were capable. The war forced men to find another voice, often more plangent and less conventional: Buchan's war poetry, too often neglected, finds a register not fully reflected in his prose, even when it quite specifically addresses the fighting (as much of it does). Those who study the literature of the war will be surprised by what is here, and will widen their outlook; those who study the role of Scotland in the war will be awakened to its literary dimension.

Hew Strachan

1914

War! The winds are sighing it,
The hill birds are crying it
   To the valley's uttermost bounds ...

from 'War'
Will H. Ogilvie

War!

After weeks of political brinkmanship during which efforts were made to avert war in Europe, on 4 August the British Foreign Secretary, Sir Edward Grey, delivered an ultimatum to Germany demanding that it terminate military action against neutral Belgium or face war with Britain. On the same day, newspapers were already predicting the outcome of the faltering negotiations. Scotland's national newspaper, *The Scotsman*, predicted that stoicism would prevail: 'At any moment Great Britain may be at war with the German Powers. Her people will accept this destiny with quiet and enduring courage.'[1]

On 5 August, *The Times* carried the headline 'War Declared'[2] and by 9 August, under the command of Sir John French, the first units of the British Expeditionary Force (BEF) landed in France. Due to strict censorship, a further week passed before an official dispatch informed the people of Britain and Ireland that the BEF, as detailed for Foreign Service, had safely landed on French soil. On 10 August *The Scotsman* published its first poem of the conflict. Penned by W. H. Ogilvie, and simply titled 'War', the last stanza declared great confidence in Scotland's role in the conflict.

> Play up, pipers of Scotland, blare to the world that waits!
> Tell them our youth and manhood stand massed by the
>   Northern Gates!
> Tell them our three joined kingdoms are fain for the
>   battle to be;
> Tell them the heart of Scotland is the readiest heart of
>   the three![3]

By the time the poem was published, the men and 40,000 horses of the BEF had disembarked in three ports – Boulogne, Le Havre and Rouen – where they were welcomed enthusiastically. The first Scottish detachment to set foot in France was the 2nd Battalion, Argyll and Sutherland Highlanders. They disembarked at Boulogne and marched to the sound of their regimental pipes playing 'Hielan' Laddie', 'Cock o' the North' and the 'Road to the Isles'. One onlooker claimed that the docks at Boulogne were 'hit by waves of khaki and tartan'. Before leaving for France, the Argylls had decided that it would be diplomatic to give a bagpipe rendition of 'La Marseillaise' on arrival. As the assembled dignitaries and local crowds watched, the Argylls formed up and the pipers gave a rousing rendition of the French national anthem. To acknowledge the bonhomie of the Scottish troops, a French brass band played a rag-time version of 'Auld Lang Syne' – the 'Auld Alliance' was secure![4]

In order to gain wider powers over national security, the Government immediately introduced the Defence of the Realm Act, 1914 (DORA). Under the new legislation, the Government had the authority to censor the press, and it did so at once. The coverage of the war in its early stages was speculative; there were many generalisations and few, if any, facts. Despite the censorship of the press, no restrictions were placed on literary contributions to newspapers so long as they contained no anti-war rhetoric. Poetry very quickly gained currency and became the preferred medium in which to express the emotions of war.

Yet not everyone was enthusiastic about the war aims: in Glasgow on Saturday 15 August, a peace rally held at Glasgow Green was attended by an estimated 5,000 men, women and children. The rally was organised by left-wing political parties and peace groups; the British Socialist Party (BSP), the Independent Labour Party (ILP) and the Glasgow Branch of the Peace Society were united in their condemnation of the war and of those who would 'exploit the people's food supply by the profiteers who pose as patriots'.[5] The mood of the country did not allow for 'unpatriotic' demonstrations, however, and the mass gathering was boycotted by the press.

Furthermore, Scotland had record-breaking 'patriotic' responses to recruitment appeals and, it was claimed, had the highest proportion of voluntary enlistments in the United Kingdom. According to the *Glasgow Herald*, in Glasgow alone 30,000 able-bodied young men enlisted during the first ten weeks of the war.[6] In Aberdeen, the evening newspaper carried a quote from the Lord Provost, claiming, 'He was proud of the splendid response to the mobilisation call, and all the citizens have the utmost confidence that our Territorial Force will play their part in the present national crisis'. There was also much column space in praise of and support for the Gordon Highlanders and, as if they guaranteed success in the new conflict, the battle honours from their previous campaigns were cited.[7]

From the outbreak of hostilities in 1914, Scottish troops took part in all the major military engagements on the Western Front. From Mons to the Marne and at the First Battle of Ypres the Scots distinguished themselves. Between August and December, 12 Victoria Crosses were awarded to Scottish servicemen, one naval and eleven army. But reports of gallantry and valour alone could not sustain public support for the war and the romanticism of sending men off to fight for 'Gallant Little Belgium' began to lose its appeal.

By December 1914 there was a discernible shift in the war poetry. At the beginning of hostilities, the prevailing tone of poetry was cheerful, patriotic and imbued with a spirit of adventure. But after four months of rising casualty figures, poetry was often tinged with doubt, cynicism and dark humour. On Christmas Eve 1914, at Number 4 Casualty Clearing Hospital, Duncan Tovey of the London Scottish was recovering from his wounds. For Tovey, poetry was his love and his therapy. His poem, 'Ten Little Sausages', said much about his personal feelings towards German 'Kultur'.

> Ten little sausages marching all in line,
> One stopped to burn a church, and then there were nine.
> Nine little sausages indulging in their hate,
> One burst himself with rage, and then there were eight.
> Eight little sausages dropping bombs from heaven,
> One dropped himself instead, and then there
>   were seven ... [8]

The poem concludes with the fate of one sausage.

By the end of the year, the belligerent nations had dug in, entrenching their armies along a 475-mile continuous line known as the Western Front. On this fighting front, Scottish women also had a role to play; they served in the Regular, Reserve and Territorial Force Nursing Services, and in various independent medical and humanitarian aid units. They also served in the Naval Nursing Service. On the home front, hundreds of fundraising appeals took place; money was collected for everything from warm winter clothing for the troops to the purchase of ambulances and hospital equipment.

It was clear that the often-quoted prediction that the war would be 'over by Christmas' was more aspirational than factual.

NOTES

1. *The Scotsman*, 4 August 1914.
2. *The Times*, 5 August 1914.
3. *The Scotsman*, 10 August 1914.
4. G. Curnock, 'Birth of a World Song', in H. W. Wilson & J. A. Hammerton (eds), *The Great War: 'I Was There'*, Part 1 (London: Amalgamated Press Ltd, 1939).
5. *Forward*, 15 August 1914.
6. *Glasgow Herald*, 15 October 1914.
7. *Aberdeen Evening Express*, 5 August 1914.
8. D. Tovey, 'Grey Kilts', *London Scottish Regimental Gazette*, 1918.

A Sough o' War

The corn was turnin', hairst was near,   [harvest]
  But lang afore the scythes could start
A sough o' war gaed through the land   [sigh]
  An' stirred it to its benmost heart.   [innermost]
Nae ours the blame, but when it came
  We couldna pass the challenge by,
For credit o' our honest name
  There could be but one reply.
An' buirdly men, fae strath an' glen   [stalwart]
  An' shepherds fae the bucht an' hill,   [sheep-fold]
Will show them a', whate'er befa',
  Auld Scotland counts for something still.

Half-mast the castle banner droops,
  The Laird's lament was played yestreen,
An' mony a widowed cottar wife
  Is greetin' at her shank aleen.   [knitting alone]
In Freedom's cause, for ane that fa's,
  We'll glean the glens an' send them three
To clip the reivin' eagle's claws,   [plundering]
  An' drook his feathers i' the sea.
For gallant loons, in brochs an' toons,   [lads, burghs]
  Are leavin' shop an' yaird an' mill,
A' keen to show baith friend an' foe
  Auld Scotland counts for something still.

The grim, grey fathers, bent wi' years,
  Come stridin' through the muirland mist,
Wi' beardless lads scarce by wi' school
  But eager as the lave to list.   [the rest]
We've fleshed o' yore the braid claymore
  On mony a bloody field afar,
But ne'er did skirlin' pipes afore
  Cry on sae urgently tae war.
Gin danger's there, we'll thole our share,   [bear]

Gie's but the weapons, we've the will,
Ayont the main, to prove again   [over the sea]
  Auld Scotland counts for something still.

1914

Charles Murray

Scotland Yet!

Furth fortune and fill the fetters.
                    Motto of the Dukes of Atholl

Achnacarry, Cameron's pride,
    Whose faith is Scotland's weal,
Sends ringing down Lochaber side
    The war cry of Lochiel!
Leave gowks to stalk and coofs to dance,   [fools, simpletons]
The Camerons are furth to France.

'Dunkeld and Menzies, Blair and Scone,
    Hae gone the ways o' men;'
On Rannoch side the harvest moon
    Lights up the harried glen,
From croft and castle, glebe and manse,
The 'Forty-twa' are furth to France!

From Inverary, north to Ross,
    The flow has run to spate,
From fen and moorland, peat and moss,
    Six lads have gone in eight;
With ache of heart but pride of glance
'Argylls and Seaforths furth to France!'

By Lochnagar, – by Dee and Don
    See Huntly, Farquhar tread!
From lodge and shieling they are gone,
    The hungry ranks are fed;
Each lass seems walking in a trance,
The Gordons gay are furth to France!

From Dunnet Head to Sands o' Dee,
    From loan and mountain pass;
The Isles are swept from sea to sea
    From Lewis round to Bass;
The pipes are filled, the horses prance,
The Guards and Greys are furth to France!

The Borderers from Berwick town,
    The Scots from deep Glencorse;
The Fusiliers from banks o' Doon,
    Light Infantry in force;
The Scottish Rifles look askance
At men who go not furth to France.

For Scotland's king and Scotland's law
    They dree'd their weird in turn   [bore their fate]
On Flodden Field and Philiphaugh,
    These sons of Bannockburn;
And now its glory to enhance
They fight with England furth in France.

....

The aged chieftain takes his way
    Slow down the stricken glen,
And speaks of fame and things agley,   [awry]
    'A few may come again,
But God was good to grant this chance
To fight for freedom furth in France.'

A. Stodart Walker

Cabhlach an Rìgh

Buaidh agus piseach ler dùthaich
'S gach tìr tha dlùth dhi an dàimh,
Biodh sìth agus sonas is saorsa
Le saidhbhreas daonnan na làimh,
Gun dìochuimhn' a chur air a' chabhlach
Tha mar chearcall dian àlainn mun cuairt,
Ga dìonadh na cadal 's na dùsgadh
Gach latha 's gach oidhche 's gach uair.

Neo-lochdach mar uain air an achadh
Fhad 's tha sìth ann am beachd ar luchd-fuath,
Ach a leumas mar fhùdar on t-sradaig
Ma rùisgear an claidheamh à truaill.
Faic iad a' gluasad san astar,
A' sgoltadh 's a' sracadh nan tonn,
Gach toiseach a' tolladh 's a' gearradh
Mar stiallas crann-àraidh am fonn.

An fhairge mhìn rèidh a tha romhpa
Ag èirigh na cnocan nan dèidh,
Borb-ghoil aig gach deireadh a' seudail
Mar uisgeachan steud-shruth nan leum.
Luchd-faire nan cladach 's nan cuantan,
Fìor bhuadhmhor, neo-luaineach, ro threun,
Dian-lurach mu bhroilleach na dùthcha
Ga cumail gu cubhaidh, gun bheud.

Tha bàs anns gach aon dhiubh an tasgadh,
Deas gu spùtadh na fhrasan air nàmh
Ge b' e àit' às an tig a' chùis-chòmhraig
No ged bhrùchdadh iad oirnn às gach àird.
Grad-leumaidh iad mach bhom buill-cheangail
Mar ghathan an dealain cho clis
Nan tigeadh an t-òrdugh tron adhar:
'Faigh, agus loisg, agus sgrios!'

The King's Navy

Victory and success to our country
And each land that toasts our health –
May she long enjoy prosperity,
Peace, freedom and wealth;
Don't forget the vehement navy,
A ring round her, keen and bright,
On guard while she sleeps and she wakes,
Every hour of the day and the night.

While our foes have peace in their minds,
Our ships are gentle as lambs in a park,
But when swords are drawn from their sheaths
They leap like gunpowder to a spark.
See how quickly they move,
How they cleave and tear the surf,
Each bow boring and cutting
Like a plough slicing the turf.

The sea is calm before them
But thrown into hills in their wake:
It glitters, fierce-boiling behind them;
Waterhorses stream through a break.
Watchmen of shore and of sea
Virtuous, steadfast and brave:
A keen jewel on the breast of the land
Guarding its honour, guiding its fate.

The ships hoard death inside them
Ready to shower over our foes
Wherever the attack will come from,
Whether from above or below.
As nimble as bolts of lightning
They'll slip their chains and deploy
If the order comes over the airwaves:
'Seek out, fire on, destroy.'

Sin thòisicheadh bùraich tur oillteil
Is donnalaich dhaoidh air gach taobh,
Ràn agus sgread nan lann-nimhe
Mar gu fosgladh Ifrinn a chraos.
'S bhiodh buaidh leis a' bhrataich ghorm-dhearg-gheal –
Nuair thigeadh a' gharbh-chath gu crìch,
Bhiodh cliù agus urram sìor-ainmeil
Aig cabhlach ghrinn mheanmnach an Rìgh.

* * *

Guma fada bhios sìth feadh gach dùthcha,
Biodh an claidheamh na dhùnadh a-ghnàth,
Teann-cheangal air iall nan con beurra,
Biodh tost air an deileann gu bràth.
Oir is cumhachdach cabhlach Rìgh Deòrsa,
Trom-lannach deagh-threòraicht' gun mheang –
'S e mo chomhairle dhlùth don Roinn Eòrpa:
Na dùisgibh an leòmhann gu feirg.

Uilleam MacCormaig (*HMS Garry*, 1914)

Then horrific chaos will follow,
An evil howling on every side,
The whine and shriek of poisoned blades,
Hell's mouth opened wide.
The red, white and blue flag will triumph
When the fighting comes to an end
And fame and everlasting honour
Will fall to the King's proud Navy men.

* * *

May each country long enjoy peace,
And the sword be kept in its scabbard,
A tight leash kept on the war-dogs,
A muzzle to silence their snarl.
King George's Navy is so mighty,
Well-armed, flawless and well-led,
My considered counsel to Europe is:
Don't wake the fierce lion from its bed.

William MacCormick (*HMS Garry*, 1914)
translated by Peter Mackay

To the Bantam Brigade (Rosebery) Royal Scots

The following lines were sold by auction at a recruiting meeting presided over by Provost Malcolm Smith, the Provost acting as 'the man with the hammer'. The Royal Scots Emergency Fund became thirty shillings the richer. Mr William Sharp, Vanburgh Place, Leith Links, was the successful bidder.

Attention! a' you young Leith chiels,   [fellows]
Wha've tried to heichten up your heels,
An' spent some clink on growin' meals,
 To raise your size;
Braw bantams clockin' in their creels
 We'll ne'er despise.

There's mony a wee bit canty chap,   [lively]
Wha some micht think no' worth a rap,
Deserves mair feathers in his cap
 Than mony a giant!
His pluck is deeper in his sap,
 An' mair reliant!

Come forrit, noo, for Auld Leith's sake,   [forward]
Ilk ane o' ye o' Bantam make,
Your apathetic speerits slake
 In Rosebery's Corps;
Then steps for Kaiser Weelum take,
 An' bolt his door!

'Restalrig' (J. B. Symons)

To Germany

You are blind like us. Your hurt no man designed,
And no man claimed the conquest of your land.
But gropers both through fields of thought confined
We stumble and we do not understand.
You only saw your future bigly planned,
And we, the tapering paths of our own mind,
And in each other's dearest ways we stand,
And hiss and hate. And the blind fight the blind.

When it is peace, then we may view again
With new-won eyes each other's truer form
And wonder. Grown more loving-kind and warm
We'll grasp firm hands and laugh at the old pain,
When it is peace. But until peace, the storm,
The darkness and the thunder and the rain.

Charles Hamilton Sorley

1915

I widnie be a German
I widnie be a spy
I'd raither be a sodger
In the H.L.I.   [Highland Light Infantry]

Children's street rhyme

The Western Front: the Spring Offensive

In March 1915, the British launched a spring offensive. Its aim was to break the deadlock which had set in since November 1914. Their objective was to take Aubers Ridge but to reach Aubers, the village of Neuve Chapelle, which had changed hands several times in the early months of the war before being secured by the Germans in November, had first to be retaken. The BEF successfully broke the German-held line at Neuve Chapelle but supplies and co-ordination problems hampered attempts to advance to Aubers Ridge. The offensive turned out to be tragic and costly both in lives and ammunition. For the 2nd Battalion, The Cameronians (Scottish Rifles), thirteen officers and 112 other ranks were killed in action and 344 of all ranks were wounded or missing. It is estimated that 40,000 Allied troops took part in the battle and that there were 7,000 British and 4,200 Indian casualties.[1]

Seven months from the start of hostilities, the battle of Neuve Chapelle exemplified the nature of the war on the Western Front: enormous losses for small gains. Working in a Base Hospital on the Western Front, Sister Millicent Bruce Peterkin from Edinburgh, serving in the Queen Alexandra's Imperial Military Nursing Service (Reserve), wrote of the casualties from Neuve Chapelle: 'some of the men have the most terrible wounds, poor wretches. They say it is perfectly awful at the front just now. Some of them also say that things are not quite as good as the papers would have us believe'.[2]

A poem titled 'Dark Neuve Chapelle', composed by the men who took part in the action and which became a song, laments the Scottish losses:

> Oh, lads of the tartan! No more you'll be turning
> To the land where your true eyes turned as you fell;
> But there's many a heart in Scotland is mourning
> The lads who are lying at dark Neuve Chapelle.

At Aubers Ridge, William Linton Andrews, news editor of the *Dundee Advertiser*, and Joe Lee, journalist, writer, poet and artist, both working for the D.C. Thomson publishing house, served in the 4th Black Watch, 'Dundee's Own'. They were joined by a considerable number of journalists, writers, artists and print workers also from Dundee; the group became known as the 'Fighter Writers'.[3] In a trench before the action at Aubers, Lee wrote a poem entitled 'The Green Grass' with the prophetic lines,

> The grass grows green on the long, long tracks
> That I shall never tread –
> Why are we dead?[4]

According to the Army Returns on the casualties, 7,433 wounded were admitted to medical units from the battle for Aubers Ridge.[5] In this action, as in so many more to follow, the total number of deaths – those killed in action, missing in action and dead from wounds – was never finally determined.

Gallipoli

In April 1915 a new front opened up in the Eastern Mediterranean, and the campaign became synonymous with military incompetence and disaster.

In October 1914, Turkey entered the war allied to Germany; in the same month, the Ottoman Turks attacked the Russians in the Caucasus mountains. The British and French were concerned that, with Turkey's entry into the war, the position on the Eastern Front would be weakened and if the Russians were defeated then a large number of German troops could be deployed to the Western Front. It was the considered view of Winston Churchill, First Lord of the Admiralty, that Russia had to be supported, which would involve opening up a new fighting front. He convinced Lord Kitchener that military action was needed and could best be achieved by gaining control over the Dardanelles straits in north-western Turkey, which separated Europe and Asia. The straits had been of strategic maritime importance since the Trojan War was fought near the Aegean entrance. The planned objective was to seize or destroy the Turkish forts on the Gallipoli peninsula, thereby securing an unobstructed water corridor; this would enable Allied ships to deliver vital supplies to the hard-pressed Russians fighting on the Eastern Front. Also, having gained control of the straits, an Allied advance could be made on Constantinople, the capital of the Ottoman Empire. It was an audacious plan which failed to take into account the geography of the Gallipoli peninsula and underestimated the determination of the Ottoman defenders. Ten months after the campaign was launched, the defeated British and Allied troops were withdrawn from the peninsula. It was both a military and a medical management scandal that resulted in 209,604 army and naval battle and non-battle casualties.[6]

Serving at Gallipoli was Lieutenant W. Sorley Brown of the King's Own Scottish Borderers (KOSB), whose war diary regularly appeared in the columns of the *Border Standard*. He was a great lover of poetry and his diary made regular reference to the poetry of the war. In one entry he wrote, 'The sonnets published below were composed in my presence by Lieutenant Maurice Lumgair'. One of the sonnets, 'Gallipoli – 12 July – 1915', honoured the men of the KOSB who died in the 12 July engagements. The first stanza laments the loss of the Bordermen, ending, 'Sweet Borderland, for thine immortal fame,/ Thy sons against the Turkish lines were borne'.[7]

In a diary entry just before the evacuation of the Gallipoli peninsula, Sorley Brown wrote, 'The fine people who wanted us to hold on to what we had gained at so terrible a cost ought to have been there to form a properly considered opinion. I say they ought to have been there; I say no more.'

The Western Front – Loos and Losses
On 25 September, the British First Army's six divisions engaged with their French allies to launch the Artois-Loos offensive. Taking part was the 15th (Scottish) Division, one of Kitchener's New Army units formed in September 1914. According to Philip Gibbs, the war correspondent, 'It was the first big attack of the 15th Division. They were determined to go fast and go far. Their pride of race was stronger than the strain on the nerves.'[8]

The offensive cost the BEF 50,000 casualties, half of them sustained by the 15th (Scottish) Division. Working in an advanced casualty treatment unit, Sister Jean Birrell from Glasgow summed up in one short diary entry the effects of the battle on the Scottish troops: 'Nothing but tartan and gore all round'. On the home front, the attack by the 15th soon developed legendary status, and such was the public's interest in the Division's engagement at Loos that the *Inverness Courier* printed a penny pamphlet with a report of the action.

The Scottish troops' first year of war was later recorded in a poem by Alice MacDonell of Keppoch, 'To the Lion Rampant'. The poem concludes:

> Gay Gordon lads, brave Seaforths, Black Watch
>   and Camerons tell,
> What steeled your dauntless hearts to face that living
>   screen of hell!
> The pipes of Loos, of Mons, of far and distant Dardanelles,
> That spake in Gaelic tones to each who dared those deadly
>   shells.
> The old time slogan of the race, the spell that cannot fail.
> 'À chlanna nan gaidheal!, 'À chlanna nan, Gaidheal!
> Guillain ri Guillain a chèile!'[9] *

* Sons of the Gael shoulder to shoulder

NOTES

1. G. Bridger, *The Battle of Neuve Chapelle* (Barnsley: Pen and Sword, 1998).

2. M. B. Peterkin, War Diary 1915, Imperial War Museum, Catalogue No.7058.

3. W. L. Andrews, *Haunting Years* (London: Hutchinson and Co., 1930).

4. R. Burrows, *Fighter Writer: The Eventful Life of Sergeant Joe Lee, Scotland's Forgotten War Poet* (Derby: Breedon Books, 2004), p.74.

5. T. J. Mitchell, *Medical Services; Casualties and Medical Statistics*, (London, 1931; Imperial War Museum and Battery Press, 1997), p.135.

6. Alan Moorehead, *Gallipoli* (London: Hamish Hamilton, 1956).

7. W. Sorley Brown, *My War Diary (1914–1919): Recollections of Gallipoli, Lemnos, Egypt and Palestine* (Galashiels: John McQueen and Son Ltd, 1941), pp. 90, 91.

8. Philip Gibbs, *Now It Can Be Told* (New York/London: Harper and Brothers. Part iv, 1920).

9. Sir Bruce Seton and Pipe Major John Grant, *The Pipes of War: A Record of the Achievement of Pipers of Scottish and Overseas Regiments During the War 1914–1918* (Glasgow: Maclehose, Jackson & Co,1920), pp.228–31.

A Recruit for the Gordons

I'm aff! The halflin gets my crib,   [boy]
   An' keeps the chaumer key;   [mens' quarters]
The morn aul' Mains can dicht his nib,   [wipe his nose]
   An' scoor the lift for me.   [scan the horizon]

I've listed! Dang the nowt an' neeps!   [cattle and turnips]
   I'm aff to fecht or fa';   [fight or fall]
I ken, withoot their weary threeps,   [nagging]
   They're mair than needin's a'.

Wi' Huns upon wir thrashel-stane,   [our threshold]
   An' half the world red wud,   [mad]
Gweed sax feet ane o' brawn an' bane,   [good]
   Is nae for plooman dud.

An' sae I paumered back an' fore,   [wandered]
   Practeesin' in my kilt,
An' Sownock fae the bothy door
   Kame-sowfed a martial lilt.   [played on comb and paper]

They leuch till howe and hill-tap rang –   [laughed]
   I steppit saft mysel', –
For aye anaith my bonnet sang
   Bit things I couldna tell –

The bonnet wi' the aul' 'Bydand'   [regimental motto]
   That sat upon my broo –
An' something stirred, grey Mitherland,
   In my puir hert for you,

As aye an' aye the plaidie green
   Swung roon my naked knee,
An', mairchin' there anaith the meen,   [moon]
   Lord Sake! That wasna me,

The eat-meat sumph that kissed the quines,   [lout, girls]
    An' took a skyte at Eel;   [drink at Christmas]
I was the heir o' brave langsynes,
    A sojer, head to heel.

Ay me! 'At never shot a craw,
    Nor killed a cushey-doo –   [wood-pigeon]
But bleed's aye bleed, an' aul' granda   [blood]
    Did things at Waterloo.

....

I'm aff the morn . . . There's nane'll ken
    O' ae broon curly head,
That ees't to lie aside my ain
    In Mains's stoupet bed: [poster-bed]

It's laich, laich noo, in Flanders sod,   [low]
    An' I'm mairchin' wi' the drum,
'Cause doon the lang La Bassée road
    There's dead lips cryin' 'Come!'

Mary Symon

'K(1)'

We do not deem ourselves A1,
We have no past: we cut no dash:
Nor hope, when launched against the Hun,
To raise a more than moderate splash.

But yesterday, we said farewell
To plough; to pit; to dock; to mill.
For glory? *Drop it!* Why? Oh, well –
To have a slap at Kaiser Bill.

And now to-day has come along.
With rifle, haversack, and pack,
We're off, a hundred thousand strong.
And – some of us will not come back.

But all we ask, if that befall,
Is this. Within your hearts be writ
This single-line memorial: –
He did his duty – and his bit!

Ian Hay

K1 was the first Army Group of Kitchener's volunteer army – the 'First Hundred Thousand'.

Only Twa!

The following lines were suggested by a letter from a resident in a certain Border town which stated that out of a large number of men employed by the Co-operative Society in that town, only two had responded to their country's call in the great conflict of 1914–15.

'Yes, that's the number, sir' she said,
　'Only twa; only twa';
And low the lassie bow'd her head,
　Only twa! only twa!
'To see the callants, sir, it's rare;　　　　　　　[lads]
They're comin' in, baith rich an' puir;
But faix, the Store can gie nae mair –　　　　　[faith]
　Only twa; only twa!

'It's true, sir, true, as sure as daith –
　Only twa; only twa;
Ye'd thocht they'd raise a score, but faith
　Only twa; only twa;
Ye'll see them there, baith big an' wee;
A pund ye ask – a pund they gie;
But as for 'listin', sir, ach me! –
　Only twa; only twa.

'I'm vex'd mysel' I'm no' a man –
　Only twa! only twa!
For sic' tame wark is bad to stan' –
　Only twa; only twa.
In times o' peace ye'll hear them sing
Wi' brazen notes, "God Save the King!"
But when it comes to fechtin' – 'twing! –　　　　[fighting]
　Only twa! only twa!

'Na, na, guid sir, I've nae friens there –
　Only twa! only twa!
If sae, I'd pu' their verra hair –
　Only twa! only twa!

Gang on ye loons an' punch yer dough;
Mairch on, ye fireside warriors, ho!
Yer no' the stuff – yer no', yer no' –
  Only twa! only twa!'

David J. Beattie

Soldier, Soldier

Wastrel, wastrel, standing in the street,
Billy-cock upon your head; boots that show your feet.

Rookie, rookie, not too broad of chest,
But game to do your bloomin' bit with the bloomin' best.

Rookie, rookie, growling at the grub;
Loth to wash behind the ears when you take your tub.

Rookie, rookie, licking into shape –
Thirty-six inch round the buff showing by the tape.

Rookie, rookie, boots and buttons clean;
Mustachios waxing stronger; military mien.

Rookie, rookie, drilling in the square,
Britain's ancient glory in your martial air.

Rookie, rookie, swagger-stick to twirl;
Waving hands to serving-maids; walking out the girl.

Soldier, soldier, ordered to the front,
Marching forward eager-eyed, keen to bear the brunt.

Soldier, soldier, bidding her good-bye –
'When I come back I'll marry you, so, darling, don't you cry!'

Soldier, soldier, sailing in the ships,
Cigarettes and curious oaths betwixt your boyish lips.

Soldier, soldier, standing in the trench;
Wading through the mud and mire, stifling in the stench.

Soldier, soldier, 'mid the din and dirt,
More than monastic tortures moving in your shirt.

Soldier, soldier, facing shot and shell;
Jesting as you gaze within the open Gate of Hell.

Soldier, soldier, charging on the foe,
With your comrade's dying cry to urge you as you go.

Soldier, soldier, stilly lying dead,
With a dum-dum bullet through your dunder head.

Soldier, soldier, with a smile of grace,
Breaking through the grime and grit on your blood-swept face.

Soldier, soldier, sound will be your sleep,
You will never waken, though you hear her weep.

Soldier, soldier –
       How I love you!

Joseph Lee

A Woman in the Street

Edina, 1915

O bonnie lad wi' the kilt sae braw
    An' tossel't sporran swingin' –
Wi' dirk at the hip, an' ribbons rid;
    Ye set my hert a-singin'.

What are ye like that's brave an' fine! –
    The Muir-cock or the Eagle?
Your bonnet sets just like a comb,
    Your pride is like the deevil!

Och! Sair I grudge ye to the trenches, lad:
    Few flesh an' bane are like ye;
Your knees are hard, your e'en are clean –
    For *you* I'd fecht – God strike me!

Ye wanton rogue! but I love your swing,
    An' weel I guess your fettle!
For a swatch o' you I'd face *my* bit –
    Proud to beget sic metal.

But there he goes; wi' never a glance:
    To that damned hell in Flanders.
My gift is nocht – his seed gangs waste –
    Curse on the cause that squanders!

Squanders the wealth of Scotland's kind,
    In their high day and flower,
While we wha hae the grace to save
    Stand Kirk-denied Love's dower.

Pittendrigh Macgillivray

Lines Before Going

Soon is the night of our faring to regions unknown,
There not to flinch at the challenge suddenly thrown
By the great process of Being – daily to see
The utmost that life has of horror and yet to be
Calm and the masters of fear. Aware that the soul
Lives as a part and alone for the weal of the whole,
So shall the mind be free from the pain of regret,
Vain and enfeebling, firm in each venture, and yet
Brave not as those who despair, but keen to maintain,
Though not assured, hope in beneficent pain,
Hope that the truth of the world is not what appears,
Hope in the triumph of man for the price of his tears.

Alexander Robertson

Hey, Jock, are ye glad ye 'listed?

Hey! Jock, are ye glad ye 'listed?
O Jock, but ye're far frae hame!
What d'ye think o' the fields o' Flanders?
Jockey lad, are ye glad ye came?
Wet rigs we wrought in the land o' Lennox,   [fields]
  When Hielan' hills were smeared wi' snaw;
Deer we chased through the seepin' heather,
  But the glaur o' Flanders dings them a'!   [mud, beats]

This is no' Fair o' Balloch,
  Sunday claes and a penny reel;   [clothes]
It's no' for dancin' at a bridal
  Willie Lawrie's bagpipes squeal.
Men are to kill in the morn's mornin';
  Here we're back to your daddy's trade;
Naething for 't but to cock the bonnet,
  Buckle on graith and kiss the maid.   [equipment]

The Cornal's yonder deid in tartan,
  Sinclair's sheuched in Neuve Eglise;   [buried]
Slipped awa wi' the sodger's fever,
  Kinder than ony auld man's disease.
Scotland! Scotland! little we're due ye',
  Poor employ and a skim-milk board.
But youth's a cream that maun be paid for,
  We got it reamin', so here's the sword!   [brimming]

Come awa', Jock, and cock your bonnet,
  Swing your kilt as best ye can;
Auld Dumbarton's Drums are dirlin',
  Come awa', Jock, and kill your man!
Far's the cry to Leven Water
  Where your fore-folks went to war,
They would swap wi' us to-morrow,
  Even in the Flanders glaur!

Neil Munro

Luach na Saorsa

Stad tamall beag, a pheileir chaoil,
Tha dol gu d' uidhe; ged as faoin
Mo cheist – am beil 'nad shraon
   Ro-ghuileag bàis?
'M beil bith tha beò le anam caoin
   Ro-sgart' o thàmh?

An làmh a stiùir thu air do chùrs',
An robh i 'n dàn do chur air iùil
A dh'fhàgadh dìlleachdain gun chùl
   An taigh a' bhròin,
Is cridhe goirt le osann bhrùit'
   Aig mnaoi gun treòir?

An urras math do chlann nan daoin'
Thu guin a' bhàis le d' rinn bhig chaoil
A chur am broilleach fallain laoich
   San àraich fhuair?
'Na eubha bàis am beil an t-saors'
   O cheartas shuas?

Freagairt

'Nam shraon tha caoin bhith sgart' o thàmh,
'Nam rinn bhig chaoil ro-ghuileag bàis,
'S an làmh a stiùir, bha dhi san dàn
   Deur goirt don truagh;
Ach' s uil' iad ìobairt-saors' on àird –
   Tron Bhàs thig Buaidh.

(1915, *a' chiad latha san trainnse*)

Murchadh Moireach

The Value of Freedom

Stop a little while, slim bullet
Going to your goal: although foolish
My question – is there in your forward rush
    A foretaste of the death-cry?
Is there a living being with a tender soul
    Already severed from rest?

The hand that directed you on your path,
Was it fated to guide you on a course
That would leave orphans without support
    In a house of grief,
And an enfeebled wife
    Heartsore, sighing and crushed?

Is it a good surety for mankind
That you should put a fatal wound, with your slim little point,
In the healthy breast of a warrior
    On the cold battlefield?
In his death-cry is there freedom
    From justice above?

Answer

In my forward rush a tender one is severed from rest,
In my slim little point there is a foretaste of the death-cry,
And the hand that directed was fated to bring
    The wretched a bitter tear;
But they are all a sacrifice to freedom from above –
    Through Death comes Victory.

(*1915, the first day in the trench*)

Murdo Murray
translated by Ian MacDonald

Òran a' Phuinnsein

Fhearaibh, a bheil cuimhn' agaibh
An là thàinig am puinnsean oirnn,
Nar seasamh anns na truinnsichean
'S gun nì ann gus ar còmhdach?

O, nach beag a shaoileamaid
Gun tigeadh nì às ùr oirnn –
An sruth tha ruith or sùilean,
'S sinn a' cùilearachd 's a' crònan.

Cha robh nì gu teanacsadh dhuinn
Ach làmh thoirt air an t-searbhadair,
'S a cheangal gus nach fhalbhadh e
Gu dearbhte mu ar srònan.

Cha shaoileamaid san àm bha siud
Gun robh am bàs cho teann oirnn –
Ar leamsa gur e meall a bh' ann
Nuair theann e nall air còmhnard.

Sabaid 's cath cha dèanamaid,
Ged nochdadh iad am fianais dhuinn;
Bha na deòir cho deuchainneach,
'S chan fhaicinn leus ach neònach.

Nam faighinn mar bu mhiannach leam,
Dhan Ghearmailt gum b' e m' iarratas –
'S e teine thighinn on iarmailt oirr',
Ga leaghadh sìos gun tròcair.

Dòmhnall Ruadh Chorùna

The Song of the Poison

Lads, do you remember
The day the poison came
As we stood in the trenches
   With nothing to protect us?

Oh, how little we thought
A new thing would come at us –
Stream running from our eyes
   As we crouched and we wheezed.

There was no way to help ourselves
Except to grab a towel
And tie it so that it would stay
   Firmly round our noses.

At that point we hadn't thought
That death was so close to us –
I had taken it for a shower
   As it drifted across the ground to us.

Fighting and battle were impossible
Had they even approached us,
So painful were the tears,
   While a weird glow was all I saw.

If I had things as I wanted
For Germany I'd ask
Fire raining from the sky on it
   To melt it without mercy.

Donald MacDonald
translated by Ronald Black

Lines Written in a Fire-Trench

'Tis midnight, and above the hollow trench
Seen through a gaunt wood's battle-blasted trunks
And the stark rafters of a shattered grange,
The quiet sky hangs huge and thick with stars.
And through the vast gloom, murdering its peace,
Guns bellow and their shells rush swishing ere
They burst in death and thunder, or they fling
Wild jangling spirals round the screaming air.
Bullets whine by, and Maxims drub like drums,
And through the heaped confusion of all sounds
One great gun drives its single vibrant 'Broum'.
And scarce five score of paces from the wall
Of piled sand-bags and barb-toothed nets of wire,
(So near and yet what thousand leagues away),
The unseen foe both adds and listens to
The selfsame discord, eyed by the same stars.
Deep darkness hides the desolated land,
Save where a sudden flare sails up and bursts
In whitest glare above the wilderness,
And for one instant lights with lurid pallor
The tense, packed faces in the black redoubt.

Written in fire-trench above 'Glencorse Wood', Westhoek, 11th April, 1915

W. S. S. Lyon

'I tracked a dead man down a trench'

I tracked a dead man down a trench,
  I knew not he was dead.
They told me he had gone that way,
  And there his foot-marks led.

The trench was long and close and curved,
  It seemed without an end;
And as I threaded each new bay
  I thought to see my friend.

I went there stooping to the ground.
  For, should I raise my head,
Death watched to spring; and how should then
  A dead man find the dead?

At last I saw his back. He crouched
  As still as still could be,
And when I called his name aloud
  He did not answer me.

The floor-way of the trench was wet
  Where he was crouching dead:
The water of the pool was brown,
  And round him it was red.

I stole up softly where he stayed
  With head hung down all slack,
And on his shoulders laid my hands
  And drew him gently back.

And then, as I had guessed, I saw
  His head, and how the crown –
I saw then why he crouched so still,
  And why his head hung down.

Written in trenches by 'Glencorse Wood', 19th–20th April, 1915

W. S. S. Lyon

Òran don Chogadh

Guma slàn do na gillean tha MacShimidh a' sireadh,
Guma slàn do na gillean tha leinne san àm;
Mo bheannachd le dùrachd air na dh'fhàg iad fo mhulad,
Oir tha móran dhiubh bhuineas a dh'Uibhist nam beann.

Fhearaibh th' aig baile 's a' céilidh nan taighean,
Ag éigheachd gach naidheachd mar tha tachairt san Fhraing,
Gur garadh gu dòigheil aig teine math mònadh,
Sann leinne bu deòin a bhith còmh' ribh san àm.

Chan ionann is mise 's an còrr de na gillean
Tha mach fon an t-sileadh a dh'uisgeachan trom,
Fo luaidhe nan Turcach 's fo shligeannan muirte
A' dòrtadh mar thuiltean gun sgur air ar ceann.

Ged gheibhinn car tacain cead sìneadh fon phlaididh,
Cha luaith' nì mi cadal – cha tarraing mi srann –
Nuair chluinneas mi 'n t-òrdugh bhith dol ann an òrdugh
Chum losgadh is leònadh, 's a' chòmhstri tighinn teann.

Nuair thòisicheas buaireas thig stoirm mu ar cluasan,
Tha 'n talamh mun cuairt dhinn air ghluasad for bonn,
Bidh gillean gun ghruaman len gunna rin gualainn
A' leagadh nan uaibhreach, 's a' bhuaidh bidh i leinn.

Bidh peileirean snaidhte mun cuairt oirnn am pailteas,
Am fuaim a' dol seachad, neo-thlachdmhor an srann;
Bidh gillean bha tapaidh a' tuiteam gun fhacal
'S iad crioslaicht' an acfhainn gu batal nan lann.

Chan ionann 's nuair b' òg mi bhith seòladh na geòla
Le mo chompanach còir a bu deòin a bhith leam,
Lem ghunna glan bòidheach 's mo chù air an t-sòile –
Nuair dhèanainn-sa leònadh bhiodh Dòmhnall 'na dheann.

A Song to the War

Here's to the lads that Lord Lovat's recruiting,
  Here's to the lads that are with us just now;
My heartfelt blessing to those they've left sorrowful,
  For many of them belong to Uist of the mountains.

O men who're at home going the rounds of the houses,
  Announcing each news of what's happening in France,
Warming yourselves happily at a blazing peat fire,
  It's we who'd be glad to be with you just now.

How different from me and the rest of the lads
  Who're exposed to the drenching of downpours of rain,
Under fire from the Turks with their murderous shelling
  Ceaselessly pouring like floods on our heads.

Though allowed now and then to rest under a blanket
  I've no sooner slept – I've not snored even once –
Than I hear the command to fall into line
  For firing and wounding, as conflict approaches.

When battle begins our ears are assaulted,
  The earth round about us moves under our feet,
Lads without sadness with guns to their shoulders
  Lay the mighty ones low, and it's we who will win.

Sharp-pointed bullets surround us aplenty,
  Their noise going past is an unpleasant whine;
Lively lads fall without uttering a word
  Though richly caparisoned for battling with blades.

Not at all like my youth when out sailing my boat
  With my dear companion who wished to be with me,
With my lovely smart gun and my dog on the sternseat –
  When I wounded a bird it's Donald would run.

Cha bhi mi ri gearan no caoidh anns an earrainn
   Ach seasaidh mi daingeann ris a' chath a tha teann
Le Gaidhil a' chruadail tha treun agus buadhach,
   Nì Turcaich a sguabadh far uachdar nam beann.

Tha sinne an earbsa ma laigheas an t-sealga
   Gun ruig sinne Stambal ged as fada e thall,
Am baile 'm bheil dòchas aig réisimeid Lòbhait
   An dramaichean òl le òran nach gann.

Mun crìochnaich mi 'n t-òran, mo bheannachd le deòin dhuibh,
   Ceud soraidh gu Flòraidh, an òigh as barraichte th' ann:
Tha mi fhathast an dòchas gun coinnich sinn còmhla
   'S air m' fhacal bidh pòg ann cur an t-sòlais gu ceann.

Pàdruig Moireasdan

I will not complain or lament at my share
  But will stand firm to face the battle that's close
With Gaels that are hardy, brave and triumphant,
  Who'll sweep away Turks from the top of the slopes.

We're confident if the bombardment dies down
  That we'll reach Istanbul though it's far over there,
The city where Lovat's regiment hopes
  To be drinking their drams with many a song.

Before ending the song, I'll send you my blessings,
  A hundred greetings to Flora, the best girl there is:
I still live in hope that we'll meet with each other
  And my word there'll be kisses to bring joy to a climax.

Peter Morrison
translated by Ronald Black

The Fallen at Gretna

O'er crimson fields and mountains steep
   They sought to roam,
Till Fate decreed that they should sleep
   Much nearer home.

But though their couch be far removed
   From scenes of strife,
Still, to the land they dearly loved
   Each gave his life.

For in the will, not in the deed,
   True courage lies;
And all had owned their country's need —
   Great sacrifice!

Max Philpot

On 22 May 1915, an estimated 214 officers and men of the 1/7th Battalion Royal Scots, and some civilians, were killed in a rail accident at Quintinshill near Gretna. The soldiers were on their way to Gallipoli.

Below

(1915)

'Great credit is due to the engine-room staff.'
                                    Admiral Beatty

The man who's down below
Sees nothing of the show;
He's only got to do his bit and wait:
With his eye upon the dial,
It's a devil of a trial
Blindly to bear the onsets of his fate.

Yes, he's buried in the deep,
And he can't have even a peep
At the things that make the blood run fast and proud:
His prison walls are thick,
And a lesser man were sick
To know he could not mingle with the crowd.

So, his colour comes and goes
And he gives a thought to those
Who are trusting to his skill and honour bright;
He reckons he is *there*,
And he doesn't turn a hair,
Though he knows he's in the bowels of the fight.

By the churning of the screw
He gets a kind o' clew
That they're jinking all they can the submarines;
For, beneath the water-line,
He can tap the secret sign,
And he has a pretty inkling what it means.

He trusts the Bridge above,
    And he thinks but little of
The dangers that beset him in his den;
    The signals tell him some,
    And he's sure there's more to come –
What, the worst? Well, it happens to all men!

    And so, within his cage,
    Oil-spray and pressure-gauge,
And drone of turbine occupy his mind:
    He doesn't see the show,
    But this we surely know,
He's the bravest man of any you can find.

John Hogben

Two Sonnets

I

Saints have adored the lofty soul of you.
Poets have whitened at your high renown.
We stand among the many millions who
Do hourly wait to pass your pathway down.
You, so familiar, once were strange: we tried
To live as of your presence unaware.
But now in every road on every side
We see your straight and steadfast signpost there.

I think it like that signpost in my land
Hoary and tall, which pointed me to go
Upward, into the hills, on the right hand,
Where the mists swim and the winds shriek and blow,
A homeless land and friendless, but a land
I did not know and that I wished to know.

II

Such, such is Death: no triumph: no defeat:
Only an empty pail, a slate rubbed clean,
A merciful putting away of what has been.

And this we know: Death is not Life effete,
Life crushed, the broken pail. We who have seen
So marvellous things know well the end not yet.

Victor and vanquished are a-one in death:
Coward and brave: friend, foe. Ghosts do not say
'Come, what was your record when you drew breath?'
But a big blot has hid each yesterday
So poor, so manifestly incomplete.
And your bright Promise, withered long and sped,
Is touched, stirs, rises, opens and grows sweet
And blossoms and is you, when you are dead.

12 June, 1915

Charles Hamilton Sorley

The Green Grass

The dead spake together last night,
   And one to the other said:
   'Why are we dead?'

They turned them face to face about
   In the place where they were laid:
   'Why are we dead?'

'This is the sweet, sweet month o' May,
   And the grass is green o'erhead –
   'Why are we dead?'

'The grass grows green on the long, long tracks
   That I shall never tread –
   Why are we dead?

'The lamp shines like the glow-worm spark,
   From the bield where I was bred –   [house]
   Why am I dead?'

The other spake: 'I've wife and weans,
   Yet I lie in this waesome bed –   [woeful]
   Why am I dead?

'O, I hae wife and weans at hame,
   And they clamour loud for bread –
   Why am I dead?

Quoth the first: 'I have a sweet, sweetheart,
   And this night we should hae wed –
   Why am I dead?

'And I can see another man
   Will mate her in my stead,
   Now I am dead.'

They turned them back to back about
   In the grave where they were laid –
   'Why are we dead?'

'I mind o' a field, a foughten field,
   Where the bluid ran routh and red   [profusely]
   Now I am dead.'

'I mind o' a field, a stricken field,
   And a waeful wound that bled –
   Now I am dead.'

They turned them on their backs again,
   As when their souls had sped,
   And nothing further said.

....

The dead spake together last night,
   And each to the other said,
   'Why are we dead?'

Joseph Lee

The Bullet

Every bullet has its billet;
　Many bullets more than one:
God! Perhaps I killed a mother
　When I killed a mother's son.

Joseph Lee

Mother

Ye were ay a rowdy laddie, Jock,
Since ever ye cam hame,
Unco ill to bed at night,
And dour to wash and kaim.   [comb]
It gave me many a he'rt-break,
To keep ye cosh and clean,   [comfortable]
Now I'm he'rt-hale sorry for't –
    Ye ken what I mean!

Your brither's deid in New Chapelle,
Your faither's in Kirkbride,
Ye're a' that's left that made for me
The joy o' Wanlochside.
I winna hae ye craven, mind,
Nor yet ower foolish keen,
Let caution gang wi' courage, lad –
    Ye ken what I mean!

If ever ye come on a German chiel   [fellow]
That looks o' landward breed,
Some harum-scarum ne'er-dae-weel,
Blae een and lint-white heid,   [blue eyes and blond hair]
That maybe played on the hairst-field
Like you when he was a wean,
Let that yin by for his mither's sake –
    Ye ken what I mean!

Nane yet got me repinin',
Nor bendin' to my load;
High heid in the market-toun,
Licht foot on the road!
There's nane to see Jean Cameron boo   [bow]
But by her bed at e'en,
And I trust you're no forgettin' –
    Ye ken what I mean!

I'm vexed noo when I think of it,
The way I let ye gang –
Just the wee clap on the shouther,   [pat on the shoulder]
And nae fareweel harangue;
I couldna look ye in the face,
For the sun was in my een,
I'm a stupid auld Scots body –
 Ye ken what I mean!

If Death were but a merchant man,
To strike a bargain wi',
The first at his booth in the Candleriggs
In the morn's morn would be me,
To swap him a fine auld withered brench
For a stubborn twig o' green –
But there! I'm only haverin' –   [babbling on]
 Ye ken what I mean!

Neil Munro

Nostra Culpa

We knew, this thing at least we knew, – the worth
Of life: this was our secret learned at birth.
We knew that Force the world has deified,
How weak it is. We spoke not, so men died.
Upon a world down-trampled, blood-defiled,
Fearing that men should praise us less, we smiled.

We knew the sword accursed, yet with the strong
Proclaimed the sword triumphant. Yea, this wrong
Unto our children, unto those unborn
We did, blaspheming God. We feared the scorn
Of men; men worshipped pride; so where they led,
We followed. Dare we now lament our dead?

Shadows and echoes, harlots! We betrayed
Our sons; because men laughed we were afraid.
That silent wisdom which was ours we kept
Deep-buried; thousands perished; still we slept.
Children were slaughtered, women raped, the weak
Down-trodden. Very quiet was our sleep.

Ours was the vision, but the vision lay
Too far, too strange; we chose an easier way.
The light, the unknown light, dazzled our eyes –
O sisters, in our choice were we not wise?
When all men hated, could we pity or plead
For love with those who taught the Devil's creed?

Reap we with pride the harvest! it was sown
By our own toil. Rejoice! it is our own.
This is the flesh we might have saved – our hands,
Our hands prepared these blood-drenched, dreadful lands.
What shall we plead? That we were deaf and blind?
We mothers and we murderers of mankind.

Margaret Sackville

'When you see millions of the mouthless dead'

When you see millions of the mouthless dead
Across your dreams in pale battalions go,
Say not soft things as other men have said,
That you'll remember. For you need not so.
Give them not praise. For, deaf, how should they know
It is not curses heaped on each gashed head?
Nor tears. Their blind eyes see not your tears flow.
Nor honour. It is easy to be dead.
Say only this, 'They are dead.' Then add thereto,
'Yet many a better one has died before.'
Then, scanning all the o'ercrowded mass, should you
Perceive one face that you loved heretofore,
It is a spook. None wears the face you knew.
Great death has made all his for evermore.

Charles Hamilton Sorley

The Glen's Muster-Roll

The Dominie Loquitur:[1] –

Hing't up aside the chumley-cheek[2],the aul' glen's Muster Roll,
A' names we ken fae hut an' ha', fae Penang to the Pole,
An' speir na[3] gin I'm prood o't – losh! coont them line by line,
Near han' a hunner fechtin'[4] men, an' they a' were Loons[5] o' Mine.

A' mine. It's jist like yesterday they sat there raw on raw,
Some tyaavin'[6] wi' the 'Rule o' Three', some widin' throu' 'Mensa'
The map o' Asia's shoggly yet faur Dysie's sheemach[7] head
Gaed cleeter-clatter a' the time the carritches[8] was said.
'A limb,' his greetin' granny swore, 'the aul' deil's very limb' –
But Dysie's deid and drooned lang syne; the *Cressy* coffined him.
'Man guns upon the fore barbette!'. . . What's that to me an' you?
Here's moss an' burn, the skailin' kirk[9], aul' Kissack's beddin 's soo[10].
It's Peace, it's Hame – but owre the Ben the coastal search-lights shine,
And we ken that Britain's bastions mean – that sailor Loon o' Mine.

The muirlan's[11] lang, the muirlan's wide, an' fa says 'ships' or 'sea'?
But the tang o' saut that's in wir bleed[12] has puzzled mair than me.
There's Sandy wi' the birstled[13] shins, faur think ye 's he the day?
Oot where the hawser's tuggin' taut in the surf o' Suvla Bay;
An' owre the spurs o' Chanak Bahr gaed twa lang[14] stilpert chiels,
I think o' flappin' butteries yet or weyvin' powets' creels[15] –
Exiles on far Australian plains – but the Lord's ain boomerang
'S the Highland heart that's aye for hame hooever far it gang.
An' the winds that wail owre Anzac an' requiem Lone Pine,
Are nae jist a' for stranger kin, for some were Loons o' Mine.

They're comin' hame in twas and threes; there's Tam fae Singapore –
Yon's his, the string o' buckie-beads abeen the aumry[16] door –
An' Dick Macleod, his sanshach[17] sel' (Guidsake, a bombardier!)
I see them yet ae summer day come hodgin' but the fleer[18]:

1. the teacher speaks; 2. fireside; 3. don't ask; 4. fighting; 5. lads; 6.struggling; 7. matted; 8. catechism; 9. church dismissed; 10. sow; 11. moorland; 12. our blood; 13. browned; 14. lanky; 15. making traps for tadpoles; 16. cupboard; 17. complacent; 18. fidgeting across the floor

'Please, sir' (a habber an' a hoast)[19], 'Please, sir' (a gasp, a gulp,
Syne wi' a rush) 'Please-sir-can- we-win-oot-to-droon-a-fulp?'[20]
...Hi, Rover, here, lad! – aye, that's him, the fulp they didna droon,
But Tam – puir Tam lies cauld an' stiff on some grey Belgian dune,
An' the *Via Dolorosa's* there, faur a wee bit cutty quine[21]
Stan's lookin' doon a teem[22] hill road for a sojer Loon o' Mine.

Fa's neist? The Gaup – A Gordon wi' the 'Bydand'[23] on his broo,
Nae murlacks[24] dreetlin' fae his pooch or owre his grauvit noo,
Nae word o' groff-write[25] trackies on the 'four best ways to fooge'[26] –
He steed his grun' an' something mair, they tell me, oot at Hooge.
But owre the dyke I'm hearin' yet: 'Lads, fa's on for a swap? –
A lang sook o' a pandrop for the sense o' *verbum sap.*
Fack's death, I tried to min' on 't –here's my gairten[27] wi' the knot –
But – bizz! A dhubrack[28] loupit as I passed the muckle pot.'
...Ay, ye didna ken the classics, never heard o 'a co-sine,
But here's my aul' lum[29] aff tae ye, dear gowkit Loon o' Mine.

They're handin' oot the haloes, an' three's come to the glen –
There's Jeemack ta'en his Sam Browne to his mither's but an' ben.
Ay, they ca' me 'Blawin' Beelie,' but I never crawed sae crouse[30]
As the day they gaed the V.C. to my *filius nullius.*
But he winna sit 'Receptions' nor keep on his aureole,
A' he says is 'Dinna haiver, jest rax owre the Bogie Roll.'[31]
An' the Duke an' 's dother[32] shook his han' an' speirt aboot his kin.
'Old family, yes; here sin' the Flood,' I smairtly chippit in.
(Fiech! Noah's? Na – we'd ane wirsels, ye ken, in '29.)[33]
I'm nae the man tae stan' an' hear them lichtlie Loon o' Mine.

Wir Lairdie. That's his mither in her doo's-neck silk gaun by,
The podduck, so she tells me, ' s haudin' up the H.L.I.
An' he's stan'in' owre his middle in the Flander's clort an' dub,
Him ' at eese't to scent his hanky, an' speak o's mornin' 'tub'.
The Manse loon's dellin' divots[34] on the weary road to Lille,

---

19. stammer and a cough; 20. get out to drown a pup; 21. girl; 22. empty; 23.
motto of the Gordon Highlanders; 24. crumbs; 25. hand-written; 26. play
truant; 27. garter; 28. sea-trout; 29. old top hat; 30. boasted so proudly; 31.
black tobacco; 32. daughter; 33. a reference to the Moray floods of 1829; 34.
Minister's son, digging the turf

An' he canna flype[35] his stockin's, cause they hinna tae nor heel.
Sennelager's[36] gotten Davie – a' moo fae lug tae lug –
An' the Kaiser's kyaak[37], he's writin', 'll neither ryve nor rug,
'But mind ye' (so he post-cairds), 'I'm already owre the Rhine.'
Ay, there's nae a wanworth[38] o' them, though they werena Loons
        o'Mine.

. . . You – Robbie. Memory pictures: Front bench, a curly pow,
A chappit hannie grippin' ticht a Homer men't wi' tow[39] –
The lave[40] a' scrammelin' near him, like bummies roon a bike[41].
'Fat's this?' 'Fat's that?' He'd tell them a' – ay, speir they fat they like.
My hill-foot lad! A' sowl an' brain fae's bonnet to his beets[42],
A 'Fullarton' *in posse*, nae the first fun' fowin' peats[43].
. . . An' I see a blythe young Bajan[44] gang whistlin' doon the brae,
An' I hear a wistful Paladin his patriot *credo* say.
An' noo, an' noo I'm waitin' till a puir thing hirples hame –
Ay, 't 's the Valley o' the Shadow, nae the mountain heichts o' Fame.
An' where's the nimble nostrum, the dogma fair and fine,
To still the ruggin' heart I hae for you, oh, Loon o' Mine?

. . . .

My Loons, my Loons! Yon winnock gets the settin' sun the same,
Here's sklates and skailies[45], ilka dask a' futtled[46] wi' a name.
An' as I sit a vision comes: Ye're troopin in aince mair,
Ye're back fae Aisne an' Marne an' Meuse, Ypres an' Festubert;
Ye're back on weary bleedin' feet – you, you that danced an' ran –
For every lauchin loon I kent I see a hell-scarred man.
Not mine but yours to question now! You lift unhappy eyes –
'Ah, Maister, tell's fat a' this means.' And I, ye thocht sae wise,
Maun answer wi' the bairn words ye said tae me langsyne:
'I dinna ken, I dinna ken.' Fa does, oh, Loons o' Mine?

Mary Symon

35. turn inside out; 36. German prison camp; 37. cake is solid; 38. worthless person;
39. mended with string; 40. the rest; 41. bees round a nest; 42. boots; 43. cutting
peats; 44. undergraduate; 45. slates and pencils; 46. carved

1916

A Vignette

On stark and tortured wire
Where refuse of war lies
Tangled in mire –
When God is flinging
Rain down the skies –
Sit three little birds, singing.

R. Watson Kerr

Verdun

On 21 February 1916, the Germans mounted an assault on the French fortress town of Verdun. Between 21 February and 26 February, the French losses amounted to 25,000 men. The German Chief of Staff, General von Falkenhayn, deduced that because of the heavy losses sustained in the 1915 engagements, the French would be unable to mount a robust defence of the fortress. In fact, to secure Verdun the French were compelled to deploy 259 out of 330 French Infantry regiments.

The French Commander, Joffre, calculated that if French casualty rates continued at the February levels, by the end of May the French army would cease to exist; therefore Allied support was required to relieve the pressure on the much depleted, worn-down French forces. The BEF would have to deflect the German attacks on Verdun by drawing them into a new offensive.[1]

Jutland

The Battle of Jutland (31 May–1 June) was fought by the British Royal Navy's Grand Fleet against the German Imperial Navy's High Seas Fleet, in the North Sea off the coast of Denmark's Jutland peninsula. It was the largest naval battle and the only full-scale clash of battleships in the war. The outcome was tactically inconclusive, but was considered to be a strategic victory for the British. The losses, however, were undeniable: 9,823 men, of whom 6,784 were British and 3,039 German.

Some of the casualties were brought to the Forth, where they were disembarked at the Hawes Pier, South Queensferry and Rosyth Naval Base. Many of the wounded were taken to the Queen Mary and Princess Christian Naval Hospital at Butlaw. A small number of the Jutland casualties who died in the naval hospital were buried in South Queensferry cemetery, where the local population raised a memorial to them.[2]

The Somme

By the summer of 1916 the British army had a new Commander in Chief, the Scotsman Douglas Haig, and he was persuaded by the French to relieve the pressure on Verdun by opening up a new front. It was agreed that the BEF and Allied troops would engage with the Germans in Picardy, northern France: the offensive would begin on the Somme. On 1 July, the British and Allied offensive began. The week before the attack, the British artillery carried out a relentless bombardment of the German front line in the belief that the German trenches and fortifications would be destroyed. One officer commented that by destroying the German dug-outs, wire entanglements and gun emplacements, the 1 July assault would be a 'cake-walk'. However, General Jack, second-in-command of the 2nd Scottish Rifles, did not believe that success would be a matter of course. His diary entry states that he had a sleepless night and rose early, shaved, but did not wash because there was not enough water. He then 'slipped on tunic, boots, accoutrements and silver spurs in order to be properly dressed for, likely enough, the last time'.[3]

Nevertheless there was an expectation among the British High Command and thousands of trusting soldiers that it would be a battle for which the ground would be so well prepared that the army would advance effortlessly; their misplaced belief turned into the worst human disaster in British military history. The German trenches were almost impregnable and despite days of bombardment their fortifications were not destroyed. Battalion after battalion was thrown into the maelstrom and British and Dominion Forces sustained 60,000 casualties on the first day of the attack: 20,000 dead and 40,000 missing or wounded.[4]

The men who fought on the Somme were the soldiers of Kitchener's new armies. They were the volunteers who, in the opening months of the war, enthusiastically signed up for war service. The ranks of the new armies were filled with thousands upon thousands of men from all classes, backgrounds, trades, occupations, professions, the unemployed and the dispossessed. On that day, the volunteers paid a heavy price; racked with bullets, mutilated by shells or hanging on uncut barbed wire they died obscene deaths. Others would later die in casualty clearing stations, base hospitals or home hospitals. Amongst the casualty figures were the men and boys of 2nd Scottish Rifles; 15th Royal Scots; 16th Royal Scots; 1st King's Own Scottish Borderers; 15th Highland Light Infantry; and the 2nd Gordon Highlanders. Additionally, the 1st and 2nd Tyneside Scottish and the 1st London Scottish fought on 1 July. The 9th (Scottish) Division Pioneers were in reserve. Such was the scale of the battle casualties that it took days for many of the men to be found, removed from the battlefield and treated.

Working as a stretcher-bearer, William St Clair from Kirkintilloch was overwhelmed by the number of wounded and by the ninth day of the battle he wrote in his diary, 'It is beyond me to describe what we are seeing just now. I don't think I shall forget anything of this experience'. By 17 July the carnage had not ended and William, now working at a dressing station, could not conceal the effect it was having on him: 'what terribly shattered men we have to attend and still they come in what seems a never-ending line of cars, which unburden their load of groaning blood-bespattered, mud-covered heroes every minute of the day and night'. He said it was 'awful' dealing with so many traumatic injuries and at times, 'despite my former gruesome experiences', he felt overcome.[5]

The short military engagement that Haig anticipated turned into 144 days of fighting and the names of Albert, Bazentin Ridge, Delville Wood, Pozières, Guillemont, Ginchy, Flers–Courcelette, Morval, Thiepval, the Transloy Ridges and Ancre Heights became synonymous with death and destruction on an obscene scale. The combined human cost of battle and non-battle casualties to the BEF on the Somme totalled 1,295,583.[6]

It did not take long for the grief and tragedy of the Somme to be expressed in national, local and personal poetry. Before war memorials could be built, Rolls of Honour, Rolls of Service and Books of Remembrance were published by towns, counties and institutions. Poetry very often accompanied the entries for local servicemen lost in the war.

One young boy from Traquair served in France for nine months and just before the end of the Somme hostilities he was killed by a shell. He was fondly remembered by his local community as quiet, hard-working and conscientious. He was a ploughman and had a strong emotional bond with his plough horse. The beauty of the relationship was remembered in the unattributed extract from a poem chosen for his entry in the *Book of Remembrance for Tweeddale*:

The horse his kindly voice controlled
(By loving tendance made his own)

Will chafe beneath a stranger's touch
And wonder at a stranger's tone.[7]

By the end of 1916, poetry, professional and amateur, became the language of grief and protest. No longer was the war thought of in terms of chivalry, heroics and patriotism; the daily casualty lists published in national and local newspapers soon brought home the realities of war as did the increasing street shrines to 'the fallen'. Words such as 'futile' crept into conversations and newspaper columns.

NOTES

1. A. Horne, *The Price of Glory: Verdun 1916* (London: Macmillan, 1962).
2. *Scotland's War 1914–1919*, University of Edinburgh, http://www.scotlandswar.ed.ac.uk.
3. J. Terraine (ed.), *General Jack's Diary: 1914–18* (London: Cassell, 1964), p.22.
4. M. Middlebrook, *The First Day of The Somme* (Harmondsworth: Penguin Books, 1984).
5. J. St Clair (ed.), *The Road to St Julien: The Letters of a Stretcher-Bearer from The Great War* (Barnsley: Pen and Sword, 2004), pp.113–15.
6. T. J. Mitchell, *Medical Services. Casualties and Medical Statistics* (London, 1931; Imperial War Museum and Battery Press, 1997), p.149. 'Battle casualties' are defined as those killed, died of wounds, missing, prisoner of war, wounded; 'non-battle casualties' refers to sickness, disease or injury not sustained in combat.
7. *The Book of Remembrance for Tweeddale, Books IV and V: Landward Parishes* [...] by Dr [Clement] Gunn (Peebles: J.A. Kerr & Co., 1925), p.70.

Prayer Before Action – 1916

Dear God, when zero time arrives
And I am in the killing stunt,
To take perhaps a dozen lives,
Or I myself to get the shunt,
Forgive me if the chaps I cop
Have something of your love in them;
And when we all meet up on top,
Temper my D.C.M.*

Dear God, if I should be napooed,   [killed]
Sent straight to walk the Milky Way,
I'll walk it better if you should
Give me a little grace to-day.
A prayer need not contain one word,
And, somehow, when I think of Christ,
A lonely road seems so absurd,
He'll meet me at the tryst.

The nations all are up in arms,
Millions of blighters shooting some;
The star-turns have mislaid their charms,
The mock-heroic harps are dumb.
It is a rotten business, and
This lad, who never was a saint,
Sighs softly for your promised land,
But takes care not to faint.

I have an instinct in my wit,
Something beyond the pride of race,
I have to do this little bit
To make the world a better place.
So when the barrage lifts, and I
Go out for hits by shells and things,
Make it an easy job to die,
And give my spirit wings.

William Hutcheson

*District Court Martial

War

The songs I've sung are futile,
Of little futile things,
Of foolish dreams and fancies
On feeble faltering wings;
So I will cease my singing,
And take you by the hand,
Down days and darksome ditches
To the night of No-man's-land.
Where the day is full of horror
That words may never tell,
And the twilight full of terror,
And life is laughing hell.
Where your body will be filth-clad,
And your soul will fade away;
Where you'll curse your only brother
As you plod the clutching clay.
You'll scramble in the muck-heap
To soothe your hunger-ache,
With your silly heart aflutter,
And your silly soul aquake.
And when your heart is broken,
And you care not if you die,
You'll keep on carrying on
Till self-pity makes you cry;
Till you take the man who loved you
And rake him through the mud,
And scoop a shallow hollow,
With your hands all smeared with blood,
And throw him in, and leave him;
And you'll laugh for – God knows why!
And you'll keep on carrying on,
(Or God loves you, and you die),
'Mong the filth and fear and hunger
In strife to fight and fend,
From ages unbeginning
To ages beyond end.

John Peterson

The Shell Hole

In the Shell Hole he lies, this German soldier of a year ago;
But he is not as then, accoutred, well, and eager for the foe
He hoped so soon, so utterly, to crush. His muddy skull
Lies near the mangled remnants of his corpse – war's furies
    thus annul
The pomp and pageantry that were its own. White rigid bones
Gape through the nauseous chaos of his clothes; the cruel stones
Hold fast the letter he was wont to clasp close to his am'rous
    breast.
Here, 'neath the stark, keen stars, where is no peace, no joy,
    nor any rest,
He lies. There, to the right, his boot, gashed by the great shell's
    fiendish whim,
Retains – O horrid spectacle! – the fleshless stump that was his
    limb!
Vile rats and mice, and flies and lice and ghastly things that
    carrion know
Have made a travesty of Death of him who lived a year ago.

France, 10th September, 1916

Hamish Mann

R.I.P.

Lay them together in this muddy shell-hole,
Cover them over with this muddy sheet.
Heed not their staring eyes, they gaze to starry skies
Wrap their red tartans around their poor feet.
Cover them quickly nor mutter a prayer,
Pile on the earth quick with never a pang,
Mark it another grave – haste, ev'ry second save –
Here on this rifle their tin helmets hang.

High soar the night flares – hush! swift to your fire-step:
Leave them to rest there out under the stars,
Boys of the city bred, men of the tartan dead,
Laid in the lone waste by sad dead Le Sars.

So do we leave you, lads, laid in the sheer waste,
Sleeping till summer shall flit o'er the foam,
Robed in her gold and blue, to clasp, caressing you,
Close to her bosom, her own gathered home.

John Peterson

The Volunteer

I took my heart from the fire of love,
    Molten and warm not yet shaped clear,
And tempered it to steel of proof
    Upon the anvil block of fear.

With steady hammer-strokes I made
    A weapon ready for the fight,
And fashioned like a dagger-blade
    Narrow and pitiless and bright.

Cleanly and tearlessly it slew,
    But as the heavy days went on
The fire that once had warmed it grew
    Duller, and presently was gone.

Oh, innocence and lost desire,
    I strive to kindle it in vain,
Dead embers of a greying fire.
    I cannot melt my heart again.

1914–1916

E. A. Mackintosh

Home

A hissing stove whose pale blue flame
Boils peeled potatoes pillaged without shame
The night before from captured village where
The Germans were, not long ago; a chair,
A wooden table; and in glimmerings shed
By one small candle's light, a wooden bed
Or two, mattressed with small heaps of straw
Or shreds of wood; and round about where paw
Of reckless conquerors has been, – wild strewn, –
A sty of food and tins and drink, all thrown
Down in picturesque disorder. Then,
Along low wood-walled passages the den,
Our German Dug-Out – leaks into the sky
By stair-cased rough-shod shafts steep and high.

R. Watson Kerr

Route March Roundelay
A Horse

Knee-deep in grasses, fetlock deep in dew,
Heart-deep in clover, full and cool and wet,
He, the Beast of Burden, watched us tramp it through
'Twixt the twining hedge-rows that bounded off his Heaven,
Layer deep in dust, blasphemy deep in sweat,
Full pack, and blanket, and a hundred of 'Mark Seven.'*

George A. C. Mackinlay

*a type of cartridge

A Memory

Red roofs peeping through the stately trees,
A distant spire; smoke floating on the breeze;
The whir of aeroplanes high overhead;
Brown cows, by dirty village girls led;
A cyclist rushing down the road in front;
And infantry, away to bear the brunt.
The shrill cry of the farmer to his mare,
A blue betrousered Frenchman over there;
The trailing cavalcade of mounted grooms,
And distant thunder where the big gun booms.
The mottled tents and blankets out to dry,
An orderly, who carries water by,
And fleecy clouds that climb the azure sky.

Maisnil-Bouché, 24 September, 1916

Hamish Mann

A Song of Winter Weather

It isn't the foe that we fear;
It isn't the bullets that whine;
It isn't the business career
Of a shell, or the bust of a mine;
It isn't the snipers who seek
To nip our young hopes in the bud:
No, it isn't the guns,
And it isn't the Huns –
It's the MUD,
      MUD,
         MUD.

     It isn't the *mêlée* we mind.
     That often is rather good fun.
     It isn't the shrapnel we find
     Obtrusive when rained by the ton;
     It isn't the bounce of the bombs
     That gives us a positive pain:
     It's the strafing we get
     When the weather is wet –
     It's the RAIN,
           RAIN,
             RAIN.

It isn't because we lack grit
We shrink from the horrors of war.
We don't mind the battle a bit;
In fact that is what we are for;
It isn't the rum-jars and things
Make us wish we were back in the fold:
It's the fingers that freeze
In the boreal breeze –
It's the COLD,
      COLD,
         COLD.

Oh, the rain, the mud, and the cold,
The cold, the mud, and the rain;
With weather at zero it's hard for a hero
From language that's rude to refrain.
With porridgy muck to the knees,
With a sky that's a-pouring a flood,
Sure the worst of our foes
Are the pains and the woes
Of the RAIN,
          the COLD,
                    and the MUD.

Robert Service

The Bombers

The Bombers make merry with primers and fuses,
But when they get busy I am full of excuses
To go – for I find in bombs nought that amuses –
    But rather the other extreme.

The bomb No. 5 with its iron serration
Arouses in me not the least fascination;
In fact I run fast when they start detonation;
    And you can't see my feet then for dust.

But still they go playing about with delight
In the midst of gun-cotton, gunpowder, lyddite,
Or throwing live bombs in the peace of the night
    And disturbing the sleep of the camp.

On account of their hobbies the Bombers we dub
The Boys who belong to 'The Suicide Club'!

France, 1916

Hamish Mann

The Sniper

Two hundred yards away he saw his head;
   He raised his rifle, took quick aim and shot him.
Two hundred yards away the man dropped dead;
With bright exulting eye he turned and said,
   'By Jove, I got him!'
And he was jubilant; had he not won
   The meed of praise his comrades haste to pay?
He smiled; he could not see what he had done;
   The dead man lay two hundred yards away.
He could not see the dead, reproachful eyes,
   The youthful face which Death had not defiled
But had transfigured when he claimed his prize.
   Had he seen this perhaps he had not smiled.
He could not see the woman as she wept
   To hear the news two hundred miles away,
Or through his every dream she would have crept,
   And into all his thoughts by night and day.
Two hundred yards away, and, bending o'er
   A body in a trench, rough men proclaim
Sadly, that Fritz, the merry, is no more.
   (Or shall we call him Jack? *It's all the same.*)

W. D. Cocker

German Prisoners

When first I saw you in the curious street,
Like some platoon of soldier ghosts in grey,
My mad impulse was all to smite and slay,
To spit upon you – tread you 'neath my feet.
But when I saw how each sad soul did greet
My gaze with no sign of defiant frown,
How from tired eyes looked spirits broken down,
How each face showed the pale flag of defeat,
And doubt, despair, and disillusionment,
And how were grievous wounds on many a head,
And on your garb red-faced was other red;
And how you stooped as men whose strength was spent,
I knew that we had suffered each as other,
And could have grasped your hand and cried, 'My brother!'

Joseph Lee

In Memoriam

Private D. Sutherland
killed in action in the German trench, May 16, 1916,
and the others who died

So you were David's father,
And he was your only son,
And the new-cut peats are rotting
And the work is left undone,
Because of an old man weeping,
Just an old man in pain,
For David, his son David,
That will not come again.

Oh, the letters he wrote you,
And I can see them still,
Not a word of the fighting
But just the sheep on the hill
And how you should get the crops in
Ere the year got stormier,
And the Bosches have got his body,
And I was his officer.

You were only David's father,
But I had fifty sons
When we went up in the evening
Under the arch of the guns,
And we came back at twilight –
O God! I heard them call
To me for help and pity
That could not help at all.

Oh, never will I forget you,
My men that trusted me,
More my sons than your fathers',
For they could only see
The little helpless babies
And the young men in their pride.
They could not see you dying,
And hold you while you died.

Happy and young and gallant,
They saw their first-born go,
But not the strong limbs broken
And the beautiful men brought low,
The piteous writhing bodies,
The screamed 'Don't leave me, Sir',
For they were only your fathers
But I was your officer.

E. A. Mackintosh

The Field by the Lirk o' the Hill

Daytime an' nicht,
   Sun, wind an' rain;
The lang, cauld licht
   O' the spring months again.
The yaird's a' weed,
   An' the fairm's a' still –
Wha'll sow the seed
I' the field by the lirk o' the hill?   [hollow]

Prood maun ye lie,
   Prood did ye gang;
Auld, auld am I,
   But O! life's lang!
Ghaists i' the air,
   Whaups cryin' shrill,   [curlews]
An you nae mair
I' the field by the lirk o' the hill –
Aye, bairn, nae mair, nae mair,
I' the field by the lirk o' the hill!

Violet Jacob

When Will the War Be By?

'This year, neist year, sometime, never,'
  A lanely lass, bringing hame the kye,   [cows]
  Pu's at a floo'er wi' a weary sigh,
An' laich, laich, she is coontin' ever   [low]
'This year, neist year, sometime, never,
  When will the war be by?'

'Weel, wounded, missin', deid,'
  Is there nae news o' oor lads ava?
  Are they hale an' fere that are hine awa'?   [healthy and whole, far away]
A lass raxed oot for the list, to read –   [reached out]
'Weel, wounded, missin', *deid*';
  An' the war was by for twa.

1916

Charles Murray

Reconciliation

When all the stress and all the toil is over,
And my lover lies sleeping by your lover,
With alien earth on hands and brows and feet,
    Then we may meet.

Moving sorrowfully with uneven paces,
The bright sun shining on our ravaged faces,
There, very quietly, without sound or speech,
    Each shall greet each.

We who are bound by the same grief forever,
When all our sons are dead may talk together,
Each asking pardon from the other one
    For her dead son.

With such low, tender words the heart may fashion,
Broken and few, of kindness and compassion,
Knowing that we disturb at every tread
    Our mutual dead.

Margaret Sackville

1917

Flanders

Two broken trees possess the plain,
      Two broken trees remain.
Miracles in steel and stone
That might astound the sun are gone.
      Two broken trees remain.

F. V. Branford

Arras

On 9 April 1917, on the Western Front, the British and Allied forces launched their spring offensive at Arras. It was preceded by a 2,800-gun preliminary bombardment. In 1916, in advance of the Somme offensive, a similar tactic had disastrous consequences: the element of surprise had gone and the Germans were prepared for the attack. This was recent history repeating itself. In the Battle of Arras the BEF and Dominion Forces sustained terrible losses for relatively small gains. The 9th (Scottish) Division, the 15th (Scottish) Division and the 51st (Highland) Division all took part in the battle and a number of Scottish battalions in other divisions were involved. In total, 44 Scottish battalions were committed to the battle. According to the daily casualty tallies kept by each unit under Haig's command, one third of the 158,660 battle casualties were Scottish. The 51st (Highland) Division alone lost a total of 214 officers and 4,382 other ranks killed, wounded and missing. As well as the Scottish battalions there were seven Canadian battalions with Scottish heritage, including the Canadian Scottish, and the Newfoundland Regiment.[1]

Salonika

On the Salonika Front, the British Salonika Force waged a battle with disease as well as with the enemy; dysentery, enteric and malaria were rife and the prevalence of venereal disease posed a big problem for the High Command. The non-battle casualties far exceeded the battle casualties and the medical and nursing services were primarily taken up with treating and nursing infectious and fever cases.[2]

Salonika was not a popular posting, so much so that a ditty was compiled about it:

> When you're dumped upon the quay at Salonique,
> And the smell that meets you there seems to speak,
> You begin to feel quite glum,
> And to wish you hadn't come,
> For there's every kind of hum in Salonique.[3]

Scottish troops posted to Salonika were The Royal Scots Fusiliers, Cameronians, Black Watch and Argyll and Sutherland

Highlanders. The Scottish poet Christopher Murray Grieve, who wrote as Hugh MacDiarmid, served with the Royal Army Medical Corps in Salonika and France and became a casualty of the war when he contracted malaria. He damned Salonika in a poem which at first praises its beauty but then reveals it to be a place where 'Syphilis in silver hides' and 'the dervish Dysentery whirls', and ends:

> By all the wounds unstanched,
> By all the dead unhymned,
> By every broken heart
> And every ruined mind –
> The eyes are opened that were blind,
> And know thee for the murderess thou art![4]

Mesopotamia

In Mesopotamia, the campaign against the Turks started in 1914. It was undertaken by a fighting force dispatched and managed by the Indian Government and its primary role in the early phase of the conflict was to protect British interests in the Persian Gulf. Initially led by Indian Army Officer General Charles Townshend, the army successfully occupied Basra and Kurna and established a presence in the Tigris Delta. By September 1915 the troops had taken the town of Kut-al-Amara, 120 miles south of the main objective, Baghdad. When the army engaged with the Turks at the Battle of Ctesiphon, however, the engagement cost the joint force over 4,000 casualties. As it fell back to Kut-al-Amara, the army lacked adequate transport, sufficient medical supplies and staff. General Townshend was advised by the government to retire further down the Tigris but he decided to stay at Kut; this was astonishingly bad judgement on his part, and the British and Indian troops were under siege for 147 days. The conditions within the besieged garrison quickly deteriorated; the troops were near starvation rations; the medical situation was appalling and there was little or no equipment or supplies to care for the sick and wounded. The garrison finally surrendered on 29 April 1916. Approximately 13,309 men gave themselves up; of those, 3,248 were Indian non-combatants, and the sick or wounded numbered 1,456. Weakened by the effects of the siege, the captured British and Indian troops were in no condition to march to the Turkish prisoner-of-war camps in Anatolia. Of the men that left Kut on 6 May, 4,250 died either on their way to captivity or in the camps.[5]

In 1915, Seaforth Highlanders embarked for Mesopotamia and were involved in various actions, including the battles at the Sheikh Sa'ad, Wadi, Hanna, Dujailia, Sannaiyat, the fall of Kut, and the capture of Baghdad. The Black Watch and the Highland Light Infantry also served in Mesopotamia. Due to the heavy losses sustained by the Seaforths and the Black Watch in 1915, the battalions amalgamated in April 1916 until July 1917, then moved to Egypt.

The lack of care of the troops in the Mesopotamia campaign became a scandal and questions were raised in the House of Commons. Lord Henry Cavendish Bentinck, Conservative MP for Nottingham South, expressed his disgust at the inadequate planning for the care of the sick and wounded in the Dardanelles and Mesopotamia and he was not alone. Public concerns and recurrent questions raised in the House of Commons about the military and medical management in these campaigns led to the establishment of Special Commissions.[6]

Home Front
On the Home Front, war weariness and scepticism had set in, but for some it was still important to record what was happening to the Scots in the various fields of military operations. One unlikely chronicler and source of information was William Murray Kilburn, who had lost his sight as a boy. Keen to tell the story of 'the Jock' and other soldiers, William met returning wounded soldiers and recorded their experiences. He then put those stories into verse and they were printed in the *North-East Lanark Gazette*. He composed at least 70 poems during the war and they were wide-ranging in subject matter; everything from patriotism at the outbreak of the war to a poem about a Balkan mule train.

What was remarkable about William Kilburn was his ability to engage with wounded and psychologically damaged men, encouraging them to tell their stories in painful detail.[7] One soldier lamented the loss of his horse after the limber was hit by a shell:

The old gun horse is down and out, down on the shell-torn
hill;
The white spume glitters through his teeth, his eyes are
glazed and still;
Beneath the shattered limber, with his fetlocks in the stream
The old gun horse is down and out, down where the hell-
fires gleam.[8]

NOTES

1. A. McEwen, Y. McEwen, *Scotland's War 1914–1919*, Scottish Enlist-
ments and Casualties Data Base, 2006–present, University of Edin-
burgh, www.scotlandswar.ed.ac.uk.

2. W. G. McPherson, *Official Histories of the Great War Medical Services*
(London: HMSO, 1923).

3. Yvonne McEwen, *In the Company of Nurses: The History of The British
Army Nursing Service in The Great War* (Edinburgh: Edinburgh Univer-
sity Press, 2014), p.156.

4. H. MacDiarmid, 'La Belle Terre Sans Merci' (1920), *Complete Poems
vol. II*, eds M. Grieve and W.R. Aitken (Manchester: Carcanet, 1994),
p.1199.

5. Field Marshall Lord Carver, *The National Army Museum Book of the
Turkish Front 1914–18* (London: Pan Books, 2004).

6. *Hansard*, House of Commons Debate, 12 July 1916, vol.84, cc.340–
41.

7. W. M. Kilburn, *A Service Rendered*. Compiled and published by his
niece, Mae McClymont, 2014.

8. 'The Gun Horse', *A Service Rendered*, pp. 86–7.

Òran Arras

'Illean, *march at ease!*
　　Righ na Sìth bhith mar rinn
A' dol chun na strì
　　'S chun na cill aig Arras;
'Illean, *march at ease!*

Tha nochd oidhche Luain
　　Teannadh suas ri faire,
A' dol chun na h-uaigh
　　Far nach fhuasg'lear barrall;
'Illean, *march at ease!*

Tillidh cuid dhinn slàn,
　　Cuid fo chràdh lann fala,
'S mar a tha e 'n dàn,
　　Roinn le bàs a dh'fhanas;
'Illean, *march at ease!*

Gus ar tìr a dhìon,
　　Eadar liath is leanabh,
Mar dhaoin' às an rian
　　Nì sinn sgian a tharraing;
'Illean, *march at ease!*

'S lìonmhor fear is tè
　　Tha 'n tìr nan geug nan caithris,
Feitheamh ris an sgeul
　　Bhios aig a' chlèir ri aithris;
'Illean, *march at ease!*

Gura lìonmhor sùil
　　Shileas dlùth 's nach caidil
Nuair thig fios on Chrùn
　　Nach bi dùil rim balaich;
'Illean, *march at ease!*

Dòmhnall Ruadh Chorùna

The Song of Arras

Lads, *march at ease!*
  The King of Peace be with us
Going to the strife
  And to the tomb at Arras;
Lads, *march at ease!*

Tonight, Monday night,
  Moving up to guard,
Going to the grave
  Where no bootlace is untied;
Lads, *march at ease!*

Some of us will return unscathed,
  Some in agony of bloody blade,
And, according to our fate,
  Some in company of death will stay;
Lads, *march at ease!*

To defend our land,
  From grey hairs to child,
Like men gone mad
  We will draw the knife;
Lads, *march at ease!*

Many men and women
  Lie awake in heroes' land
Waiting for the news
  That the clerk has to tell;
Lads, *march at ease!*

Many an eye will weep
  Profusely without sleep
When word comes from the Crown
  That their lads won't be expected;
Lads, *march at ease!*

Donald MacDonald
translated by Ronald Black

The Corpse

It lay on the hill,
A sack on its face,
Collarless,
Stiff and still,
Its two feet bare
And very white;
Its tunic tossed in sight
And not a button there –
Small trace
Of clothes upon its back –
Thank God! it had a sack
Upon its face!

R. Watson Kerr

Any Private to Any Private

July, 1917

The speaker pointed out that owing to the number of young married men who were being killed, widows were becoming a great burden to the State – Daily Paper

Our boys are wonderful. They are always able to laugh – Daily Paper

Ay, gie's ma rum. I'm needin't sair, by God!
We've juist been bringin' Wullie doun the line –
Wullie, that used tae be sae smairt an' snod.   [neat]
Hell! what a mess! Saft-nosed ane. Damn the swine!
They micht kill clean. I kent his auld fouk fine.
Ay, he was mairrit. Man, she's spared a sicht.
Here, Dave, gie's ower that blanket. Ay, that's mine.
I kenna, hoo I canna lauch the nicht.   [laugh]

We gaed tae Tamson's schule. A clever loon   [lad]
Was Wullie. He was makin' money tae.
A'body liked him round about the toun.
Fitba'? Losh, ay! He was a de'il tae play.
We joined thegither for a bob a day;
An' noo he's deid. Here, Davie, gie's a licht.
They'll pit it in the papers. Weel they may!
I kenna, hoo I canna lauch the nicht.

I canna mak' it oot. It fair beats a',
That Wullie has tae dee for God kens what.
An' Wullie's wife'll get a bob or twa,
Aifter they interfere wi' what she's got .
They'll pester her, and crack a dagoned lot;
An' Heaven kens, they'll lave her awfu' ticht.
'A burden to the State.' Her Wullie's shot.
I kenna, hoo I canna lauch the nicht.

Envoi

What's that? Anither workin' pairtie, noo,
At six? Ay, sergeant, I'll be there a' richt.
Weel, Wullie lad, they winna wauken you.
I kenna, hoo I canna lauch the nicht.

J. B. Salmond

Conscript – 1917

I'm out because I had to come;
I am no blooming volunteer
Who fights for King and Christendom –
I jinked the army for two year.
At last they nabbed me, and, bejeeze,
They put me through the blinking mill –
' 'Shun, right turn!' no sweet, 'If you please,
Move up there, and remain quite still.'

I'm in a damned trench with full kit,
A Short Lee-Enfield with a spike;
God knows how I am sticking it,
It's not the blasted job I like.
Some one shall pay, you may be sure;
I'll do my bit and plug some lout –
A Prussian pig or Saxon boor,
I'll lay some blistered Jerry out.

To-morrow we move up, and I
Don't care a continental dam
For new ideals, but I'll die
Doing my bit, just as I am.
I may be pipped; but if I'm not
I hope to kill a dozen swine,
And D.C.M.'s*, and all that rot,
Can go to hell – the dead are mine.

William Hutcheson

* D.C.M. [District Court Martial]

Ghosts of War

(Sent from France in October, 1917)

When you and I are buried
With grasses over head,
The memory of our fights will stand
Above this bare and tortured land,
We knew ere we were dead.

Though grasses grow on Vimy,
And poppies at Messines,
And in High Wood the children play,
The craters and the graves will stay
To show what things have been.

Though all be quiet in day-time,
The night shall bring a change,
And peasants walking home shall see
Shell-torn meadow and riven tree,
And their own fields grown strange.

They shall hear live men crying,
They shall see dead men lie,
Shall hear the rattling Maxims fire,
And see by broken twists of wire
Gold flares light up the sky.

And in their new-built houses
The frightened folk will see
Pale bombers coming down the street,
And hear the flurry of charging feet,
And the crash of Victory.

This is our Earth baptizèd
With the red wine of War.
Horror and courage hand in hand
Shall brood upon the stricken land
In silence evermore.

E. A. Mackintosh

Death

Because I have made light of death
And mocked at wounds and pain,
The doom is laid on me to die –
Like the humble men in days gone by –
That angered me to hear them cry
For pity to me in vain.

I shall not go out suddenly
As many a man has done.
But I shall lie as those men lay –
Longing for death the whole long day –
Praying, as I heard those men pray,
And none shall heed me, none.

The fierce waves will go surging on
Before they tend to me.
Oh, God of battles I pray you send
No word of pity – no help, no friend,
That if my spirit break at the end
None may be there to see.

E. A. Mackintosh

Mines

(Sent from France in November, 1917)

What are you doing, Sentry,
Fresh-faced and brown?
Waiting for the mines, Sir,
Sitting on the mines, Sir,
Just to keep them down.
Mines going up, and no one to tell for us
Where it will be, and may be it's as well for us,
Mines, going up. Oh, God, but it's hell for us,
Here with the bloody mines.

What are you doing, Sentry,
Cold and drawn and grey?
Listening to them tap, Sir,
Same old tap, tap, tap, Sir
And praying for the day.
Mines going up, and no one can say for us
When it will be; but they are waiting some day for us,
Mines going up – oh! Folk at home, pray for us
Here with the bloody mines.

Where are you lying, Sentry?
Wasn't this your place?
Down below your feet, Sir,
Below your heavy feet, Sir,
With earth upon my face.
Mines gone up, and the earth and the clod on us –
Fighting for breath – and our own comrades trod on us.
Mines gone up – Have pity, oh God! on us,
Down in the bloody mines.

E. A. Mackintosh

The Scout-Fighter

He, the perfect pilot, knows
The lift of every wind that blows
Along the aerial street.
He, high Heaven's arch-athlete,
Trembles on the perilous keys
Of Death's unmortal ecstasies,
Weaving out of rushing fears
The stable rhythm of the spheres.

F. V. Branford

The Pilot

He is liege of wind and the thunder,
And desperate resolute things.
   On the market-skies
   His spirit buys
A drink of death on desolate wings.
    His hands
    Hold Fate.
    He stands
    Like Hate
Between the winds and under
   The flashing brim
   Of the waters, slim
U boats wilt at the sign of him.

He rides the wild cloud-horses
On tracks of polar gold.
   His heart is hound
   Of the hunting-ground
Where the ghostly stags are foaled.
    Through hives
    Of stars,
    He drives
    His cars
Along moon-metalled courses.
   His feet are shod
   With lightning-rod,
To walk the living hand of God.

F. V. Branford

To a Clerk, Now at the Wars

Here at your desk I sit and work,
As once you used to do;
I wonder if you'll ever guess
How much I envy you.

You'll win a world I'll never know,
Who ride the barriers down;
And my life's bounded by a desk,
And the grey streets of a town.

May Wedderburn Cannan

In the Canteen

(National Shell-filling Factory, Hayes, August, 1917)

It seems as if a long eternity
Since man was, or the world for men,
I've sweltered here. 'Way down in Tennessee,' –
One broken note pricking the air; and then
The dishes' chorus, – clatter, clitter, clatter;
The high-pitched talk, the sirens shrilling louder
Deaden the brain: I see the gravy spatter,
The puddings steam, the saucers swim in tea;
And faces, hands and necks, once fair to see,
Yellow as sea-sand with the poison-powder!
A down train rumbles: ('It's a long, long trail' –
Played in the treble half the notes are wrong.)
Up in the August gloaming, primrose-pale,
An aeroplane drones like a pagan gong.
Once more the piano twinkles through the chatter,
Poppies are dancing gaily debonair
In lazy lanes and meadows – yet what matter?
('For every Tommy has his girl somewhere.')
First stars gleam forth like pansies, till the song
Strikes deeper than the laden heart can bear!

Jean Guthrie-Smith

Home Thoughts from Abroad

Aifter the war, says the papers, they'll no be content at hame,
The lads that hae feucht wi' death twae 'ear i' the
    mud and the rain and the snaw;
For aifter a sodger's life the shop will be unco tame;
They'll ettle at fortune and freedom   [try]
    in the new lands far awa'.

No me!
By God! No me!
Aince we hae lickit oor faes
And aince I get oot o' this hell
For the rest o' my leevin' days
I'll mak a pet o' mysel'.
I'll haste me back wi' an eident fit   [diligent pace]
And settle again in the same auld bit.
And oh! the comfort to snowk again   [sniff]
The reek o' my mither's but-and-ben,   [cottage]
The wee box-bed and the ingle neuk   [chimney-corner]
And the kail-pat hung frae the chimley-heuk! [cabbage-pot]
I'll gang back to the shop like a laddie to play
Tak doun the shutters at skreigh o' day,   [day-break]
And weigh oot floor wi' a carefu' pride,
And hear the clash o' the countraside.   [gossip]
I'll wear for ordinar' a roond hard hat,
A collar and dicky and black cravat.
If the weather's wat I'll no stir ootbye
Wi'oot an umbrella to keep me dry.
I think I'd better no tak a wife –
I've had a' the adventure I want in life. –
But at nicht, when the doors are steeked, I'll sit, [shut]
While the bleeze loups high frae the aiken ruit, [log]
And smoke my pipe aside the crook.
And read in some douce auld-farrant book;   [old-fashioned]
Or crack wi' Davie and mix a rummer,   [chat]
While the auld wife's pow nid-nods in slum'er;
And hark to the winds gaun tearin' by
And thank the Lord I'm sae warm and dry.

When simmer brings the lang bricht e'en,
I'll dauner doun to the bowling-green,   [wander]
Or delve my yaird and my roses tend   [dig]
For the big floo'er-show in the next back-end.   [autumn]
Whiles, when the sun blinks aifter rain,
I'll tak my rod and gang up the glen;
Me and Davie, we ken the pules
Whaur the troot grow great in the hows o' the hills;
And, wanderin' back when the gloamin' fa's   [twilight falls]
And the midges dance in the hazel shaws,
We'll stop at the yett ayont the hicht   [gate]
And drink great wauchts o' the scented nicht,   [draughts]
While the hoose lamps kin'le raw by raw
And a yellow star hings ower the law.   [hill]
David will lauch like a wean at a fair
And nip my airm to mak certain shure
That we're back frae yon place o' dule and dreid, [sorrow]
To oor ain kind warld –

                        But Davie's deid!
Nae mair gude nor ill can betide him.
We happit him doun by Beaumont toun,   [buried]
And the half o' my hert's in the mools aside him. [earth]

1917

John Buchan

War, The Liberator

(To the Authoress of 'Non-Combatants')

Surely War is vile to you, you who can but know of it,
Broken men and broken hearts, and boys too young to die,
You that never knew its joy, never felt the glow of it,
Valour and the pride of men, soaring to the sky.
Death's a fearful thing to you, terrible in suddenness,
Lips that will not laugh again, tongues that will not sing,
You that have not ever seen their sudden life of happiness,
The moment they looked down on death, a cowed and beaten
    thing.

Say what life would theirs have been, that it should make you
    weep for them,
A small grey world imprisoning the wings of their desire?
Happier than they could tell who knew not life would keep for
    them
Fragments of high Romance, the old Heroic fire.
All they dreamed of childishly, bravery and fame for them,
Charges at the cannon's mouth, enemies they slew,
Bright across the waking world their romances came for them,
Is not life a little price when our dreams come true?

All the terrors of the night, doubts and thoughts tormenting us,
Boy-minds painting quiveringly the awful face of fear,
These are gone forever now, truth is come contenting us,
Night with all its tricks is gone and our eyes are clear.
Now in all the time to come, memory will cover us,
Trenches that we did not lose, charges that we made,
Since a voice, when we first heard the shells go shrilling over us,
Said within us, 'This is Death – and I am not afraid!'

Since we felt our spirits tower, smiling and contemptuous,
O'er the little frightened things, running to and fro,
Looked on Death and saw a slave blustering and presumptuous,
Daring vainly still to bring Man his master low.

Though we knew that at the last, he would have his lust of us,
Carelessly we braved his might, felt and knew not why
Something stronger than ourselves, moving in the dust of us,
Something in the Soul of Man still too great to die.

E. A. Mackintosh

1918

Summing Up!

When our wrath is expended,
When the world war is ended,
    It seems like to me
    That this old earth will be
More broken than mended.

Joseph Lee

No. V *from*
'Nocturnals: Tommy's Night Thoughts in the
Trenches'

1918

The conflict that started in Europe in August 1914 had by 1918 developed into a global war. After four years of unremitting losses and great hardship, the world had grown weary, and the common question had become 'when will the slaughter be over?' The belief in 1914 that it could be over 'before the leaves fall' had been shattered by overwhelming evidence to the contrary. In France alone 300,000 of her sons became casualties before the end of 1914. Amongst the Allies, Russia and France possessed the largest reserve of men for the war effort and they paid a considerable human cost for the 'Balkan Quarrel'. The two lives taken by the assassination of the heir-presumptive to the Habsburg Monarchy and his wife in Sarajevo on 28 June 1914 had been paid for by millions of lives lost before the Armistice was finally signed in November 1918.

Throughout the war, the regulars, reserves and volunteers serving in the Scottish regiments and divisions had distinguished themselves as effective and formidable soldiers, and their reputation was further reinforced and secured in the 1918 engagements and the final drive to end the war.

The spring of 1918 saw the Germans launch a death-or-glory offensive in a bid to break the Allied defences. Every type of weapon was marshalled for the destruction of the Allied Forces in the belief that this was to be the final push to secure a German victory. The offensive was codenamed 'Operation Michael', one of the four in the *Kaiserschlacht*, 'the Kaiser's Battle'. On 21 March on a 50-mile line between Arras and La Fère, the German divisions massed for an attack on the British 3rd and 5th Armies. Never before had the British line been held with so few men and so few guns (artillery) to the mile.[1]

The 51st (Highland) Division, the 15th (Scottish) Division and the 9th (Scottish) Division were involved in the first engagements and the fighting was ferocious. Within a four-hour period on the first day of the offensive, the Germans fired 1,000,000 shells. The War Diary entry of the 7/8th King's Own Scottish Borderers described the barrage as like 'the lid being taken off hell'.[2]

Between March and April the intensity of the German assault and advance did not abate. The German High Command was desperate to accomplish an all-out victory before United States forces entered the war, General Ludendorff recognising that, with the arrival of thousands of new troops from America, the tide of fortune would turn in favour of the Allies. With Russia in turmoil and effectively out of the war, Ludendorff had been able to transfer 54 divisions from the Eastern to the Western Fronts between November 1917 and March 1918, and by mid-July the German Empire reached to its greatest extent – but it was over-extended, with huge troop losses, and the first wave of the influenza epidemic was rife in the summer.

In April the 52nd (Lowland) Division had arrived to join the 3rd Army on the Western Front after traumatic campaigns in Gallipoli, Egypt and Palestine. An officer from the Division probably expressed the sentiments of thousands of men when he wrote, of the signing of the Armistice on November 11th:

> Strange to relate there was no tremendous excitement . . . Perhaps we had been fed on rumours so often that we took this for one. Perhaps we were too weary in mind and body to grasp the significance of this stupendous news. Or was it that our thoughts turned at this time to those good men who had given their lives for this great end?[3]

Between 1914 and 1918, 65 million troops were mobilised by the belligerent nations. It is estimated that around ten million were killed and twice that number wounded, and that civilian casualties were of the order of 6.6 million. It is widely believed that Scotland lost more fighting men per head of the population than any of the other nations, barring Serbia and Turkey, but this assertion has still to be verified. Certainly Scotland's losses were considerable for the size of its population.

There is no doubt, however, that the men and women of Scotland contributed greatly to the success of military campaigns, pioneered great advances in military and civilian medicine and surgery, contributed substantially to international humanitarian aid, and raised and donated millions of pounds in public giving and philanthropy. Robert Burns's ideal of a shared humanity was still at Scotland's heart.

Many of the poets had never closed their hearts to the enemy and were only too aware of shared hopes and fears between men who were fighting each other to the death. Hopes of a better world after the war ended were universal, and the soldier poets who had seen the worst were loudest in their exhortations to build upon common humanity to establish lasting peace.

Charles Hamilton Sorley, who was killed in the Battle of Loos in 1915, had written very early in the war of the hope that love rather than hatred would prevail when the armistice came, but he was in no doubt about what was to come before peace could arrive:

When it is peace, then we may view again
With new-won eyes each other's truer form
And wonder. Grown more loving-kind and warm
We'll grasp firm hands and laugh at the old pain,
When it is peace. But until peace, the storm
The darkness and the thunder and the rain.[4]

NOTES

1. J. E. Edmonds, *British Official History, Military Operations: France and Belgium 1918, Vol.1* (1935).

2. National Archives, WO95/1953, War Diary, 7/8th King's Own Scottish Borderers.

3. R. R. Thompson, *The Fifty Second (Lowland) Division 1914–1918* (Glasgow, 1923), p.572.

4. C. H. Sorley, *Marlborough and Other Poems* (Cambridge University Press, 1916).

Sonnets in Captivity

III

Endurance! That's the one outstanding wonder!
What finely tempered steel we mortals are!
What man endures! What trials he goes under
When tested in the crucible of War,
And all the unknown strength and hardihood
Latent within him is made manifest!
We had not guess'd that our frail flesh and blood
Contained the metal to withstand such test.
There is an essence of the spirit when
The soul is strong within us which imparts
To wearied bodies something of its blaze;
Strength lies not then in sinews but in hearts.
Comrades, was it not something in those days
To be a man and to endure with men?

IV

Talk not to me of courage as do some
Who speak of valour as a thing unique
Held by the Briton only. Where the drum
Beats for the martial muster you may seek
And find the brave in men of every zone.
Courage is man's distinction o'er the brute.
The brute has courage, but 'tis man alone
Fears and goes forward grimly resolute.
Thus holds he his supremacy and leads.
Who with false pride would scoff at valiant foes
Belittles all his species; let us glory
Not in the deeds we do when nations close
In the mad welter of a grapple gory,
But in the impulse which controls our deeds.

V

O God! that men could love as they can hate!
There is a gospel that is sane and pure,
And we must learn its message soon or late;
Love is the only law that shall endure.
Had all this mighty effort to destroy
Been one united effort to create
An earth to vie with paradise for joy,
What glorious vision could we contemplate!
The world has dreamed it and the world awakes!
Brothers, when Peace, compassionate, hath come,
And the hot-throated cannon silent stands,
Remember those who fell upon the Somme,
Whose bones are bleaching on Assyrian sands,
And build a nobler world for their sakes.

Enger, by Minden, Westphalia, *March 1918*

W. D. Cocker

From the Line

Have you seen men come from the Line,
Tottering, doddering, as if bad wine
Had drugged their very souls;
Their garments rent with holes
And caked with mud
And streaked with blood
Of others, or their own;
Haggard, weary-limbed and chilled to the bone,
Trudging aimless, hopeless, on
With listless eyes and faces drawn
Taut with woe?

Have you seen them aimless go
Bowed down with muddy pack
And muddy rifle slung on back,
And soaking overcoat,
Staring on with eyes that note
Nothing but the mire
Quenched of every fire?

Have you seen men when they come
From shell-holes filled with scum
Of mud and blood and flesh,
Where there's nothing fresh
Like grass, or trees, or flowers,
And the numbing year-like hours
Lag on – drag on,
And the hopeless dawn
Brings naught but death, and rain –
The rain a fiend of pain
That scourges without end,
And Death, a smiling friend?

Have you seen men when they come from hell?
If not, – ah, well
Speak not with easy eloquence
That seems like sense
Of 'War and its Necessity'!
And do not rant, I pray,
On 'War's Magnificent Nobility'!

If you've seen men come from the Line
You'll know it's Peace that is divine!
If you've not seen the things I've sung –
Let silence bind your tongue,
But, make all wars to cease,
And work, and work for Everlasting Peace !

R. Watson Kerr

On Revisiting the Somme

If I were but a Journalist,
And had a heading every day
In double-column caps, I wist
I, too, could make it pay;

But still for me the shadow lies
Of tragedy. I cannot write
Of these so many Calvaries
As of a pageant fight;

For dead men look me through and through
With their blind eyes, and mutely cry
My name, as I were one they knew
In that red-rimmed July;

Others on new sensation bent
Will wander here, with some glib guide
Insufferably eloquent
Of secrets we would hide –

Hide in this battered crumbling line
Hide in these promiscuous graves,
Till one shall make our story shine
In the fierce light it craves.

J. E. Stewart

Spring, 1918

The walnut buds in April,
The apple blooms in May,
And I will take my baby out
Under the trees to-day
And sitting there I'll say
'Next year, next year . . . '
Will the war be over
Before the sheep are shorn,
Before they cut the hay,
Before they cut the clover,
Before they cut the corn,
Or not before November
Or next year, next year?

Oh baby buds are soft, are sweet,
And baby beasts can run,
But baby boys and baby girls
Lie blinking in the sun.
Their mammies and their grannies
Have brought them in and out,
And rocked them in their cradles
And carried them about,
For months and months of war,
For daddies at the war,
In April or November.
But oh, can you remember
The times that went before?
And next year, next year . . .

Naomi Mitchison

The Armistice

In an Office, in Paris

The news came through over the telephone:
All the terms had been signed: the War was won:
And all the fighting and the agony,
And all the labour of the years were done.
One girl clicked sudden at her typewriter
And whispered, 'Jerry's safe', and sat and stared:
One said, 'It's over, over, it's the end:
The War is over: ended': and a third,
'I can't remember life without the war'.
And one came in and said, 'Look here, they say
We can all go at five to celebrate,
As long as two stay on, just for today.'

It was quite quiet in the big empty room
Among the typewriters and little piles
Of index cards: one said, 'We'd better just
Finish the day's reports and do the files.'
And said, 'It's awf'lly like *Recessional*,
Now when the tumult has all died away.'
The other said, 'Thank God we saw it through;
I wonder what they'll do at home today.'
And said, 'You know it will be quiet tonight
Up at the Front: first time in all these years,
And no one will be killed there any more',
And stopped, to hide her tears.
She said, 'I've told you; he was killed in June.'
The other said, 'My dear, I know; I know . . .
It's over for me too . . . My Man was killed,
Wounded . . . and died . . . at Ypres . . . three years ago . . .
And he's my Man, and I want him,' she said,
And knew that peace could not give back her Dead.

May Wedderburn Cannan

The Soldier's Wife

My warrior comes from France to-night
And I, so long disconsolate,
Once more the well-beloved of Fate,
With work-scarred hands go quick to light
The red fire in the polished grate,
To set the chairs and china straight;
Turned young again, with youth's delight
With happy dreams intoxicate;
I have a home again – a mate.
The centre of a world blown bright,
I wait – and wonder while I wait
My warrior comes from France to-night!

. . . And two doors down the street, alone
A woman lies, unreconciled
To grief, whose heart beat like mine own;
Whose love came back, yet came not, grown
A stranger to her and her child.
She only said he had 'gone wild,
Clean wild': and with her life turned stone
She watched this man, not hers, and smiled.

. . . And yet another tries to break
Pain's barrier of silence, wears
Her sorrow like a rose to shake
To life his dead, dead laughter; cares
For naught but this, to hear him make
The old, dear jokes; yet cannot wake
For all her eagerness and prayers
The silent boy who stares and stares . . .

I wait – and wonder while I wait.
My lamps are lit, my door ajar;
He nears, and yet he seems as far
And further than he was of late.
Like flower to flower and star to star
Were we; and yet how strange things are
To wait – and wonder while I wait!

Jean Guthrie-Smith

Raoir Reubadh an *Iolaire*

’S binn sheinn i, a’ chailin,
A-raoir ann an Leòdhas,
I fuineadh an arain
Le cridhe làn sòlais
Air choinneamh a leannain
Tha tighinn air fòrladh:
Tighinn dhachaigh thuic’ tèaraint’,
    Fear a gràidh.

Tha ’n cogadh nis thairis,
’S a’ bhuaidh leis na fiùrain
Tha nochd ri tigh’nn dhachaigh;
Tha ’n *Iolair* gan giùlain.
Chuir mòine mun tein’ i
’S an coire le bùrn air:
Ghràidh, chadal cha tèidear
    Gus an lò.

Bidh iadsan ri ’g aithris
’S bidh sinne ri ’g èisteachd
Ri euchdanaibh bhalaich
Na mara ’s an fhèilidh;
’S na treun-fhir a chailleadh,
A thuit is nach èirich –
O liuth’d fear deas, dìreach
    Chaidh gu làr!

Cluinn osnaich na gaoithe!
O, cluinn oirre sèideadh!
’S ràn buairte na doimhne –
O, ’s mairg tha, mo chreubhag,
Aig muir leis an oidhch’ seo
Cath ri muir beucach:
Sgaoil, *Iolair*, do sgiathaibh
    ’S greas lem ghràdh.

Last Night the *Iolaire* Was Torn

The lassie sang sweetly
in Lewis last night,
baking her bread
with a heart full of light
and thoughts of her darling,
longing for the sight
of her true love
    come safely home.

The war is now over,
won by the heroes
who come home tonight:
the *Iolaire*'s cargo.
Put peat on the fire
and tea from the jar; Oh,
I'll not sleep, sweetheart,
    'til morning comes.

They'll tell their tales
and we'll listen to them,
to the feats of the sea-faring
tartan-clad men;
of the brave ones who fell
and will not rise again,
so many fine lads
    who were brought down.

Hear the wind moaning –
Oh, hear it blow,
hear the sea's mocking cry
come from the depths below.
The poor lads who must battle
the sea and the foam!
Spread your wings, *Iolaire*,
    haste with my love.

Ri 'g èirigh tha 'n latha
'S ri tuiteam tha dòchas;
Air an t-slabhraidh tha 'n coire
Ri pìobaireachd brònach;
Sguir i dhol chun an dorais
'S air an teine chur mòine;
Cluinn cruaidh-fhead na gaoithe
    A' caoidh, a' caoidh.

Goirt ghuil i, a' chailin,
Moch madainn a-màireach
Nuair fhuair i san fheamainn
A leannan 's e bàthte,
Gun bhrògan mu chasan
Mar chaidh air an t-snàmh e;
'N sin chrom agus phòg i
    A bhilean fuar.

Raoir reubadh an *Iolair*,
Bàtht' fo sgiathaibh tha h-àlach;
O na Hearadh tha tuireadh
Gu ruig Nis nam fear bàna.
O nach tug thu dhuinn beò iad,
A chuain, thoir dhuinn bàtht' iad,
'N sin ri do bheul cìocrach
    Cha bhi ar sùil.

Murchadh MacPhàrlain

As the day breaks
our hope fades away,
the kettle on the chain
pipes a sorrowful lay;
she stops going to the door
with more peats for the flame;
hear the wind's harsh whistle:
    Ochone, Ochone.

The lassie wept sorely;
in the morning they found,
lying in the seaweed,
her love's body, drowned,
without shoes on his feet
as they brought him aground;
she bent down and kissed
    his lips so cold.

Last night the *Iolaire* was torn,
her brood drowned at the oars;
from Harris to Ness
our fair soldiers we mourn.
Since you won't bring them live
bring them drowned to our shores;
to the sea's hungry mouth
    we'll look no more.

Murdo MacFarlane
translated by Niall O'Gallagher

The Gaelic word 'iolaire' means 'eagle'.

AFTER THE WAR

It was 'When the War is over
Our dreams will all come true,
When the War is over
I'll come back to you';
And the War is over, over,
And they never can come true.

from 'For a Girl',
May Wedderburn Cannan

War, the Home Front and Women

In 1914, when the BEF marched off to France and Belgium, the daughters of Scotland wasted no time in mobilising their contribution to the war effort. Within days, women from all social backgrounds set to work organising 'Comfort Funds' for the troops. It was an unspoken expectation that those who could not donate money would give their time and at the outbreak of the war there was no shortage of women diligently producing comfort garments for the troops. It was estimated that 300,000 woollen belts and socks were needed for the men of the BEF.

Knitting became an almost universal response by women and schoolchildren to the war effort. Clothing and comforts collection depots were organised around the country; between August and December 1914 a quarter of a million garments were collected in Scotland and dispatched to hospitals and hospital ships. The common mantra in the early months of the war was, 'those who cannot nurse can sew', and it was taken to heart with an over-abundant enthusiasm. Ben Morrison from Shetland, who served in Palestine, wrote a poem on Shetland's 'fair daughters' knitting 'sox and gravets' for the lads:

'Plain and purl, purl and plain'
Winds loud may blow, fall sleet or rain . . .
Needles clink to this soft refrain
'Plain and purl, purl and plain'.[1]

The most obvious task women were expected to fulfil was to encourage their men-folk to 'join the colours', and thereafter wives, daughters, sisters and lovers were to provide the emotional and material comforts needed to sustain life on active service. As a result, the Active Service League established by Baroness Orczy, author of *The Scarlet Pimpernel*, came to prominence. Women of the League were pledged to encourage all able-bodied men to enlist, and took an oath stating they were 'never to be seen in public with any man who, in every way being fit and free for service, has refused to respond to his country's call'. The tactic of emotional blackmail used by the unofficial recruiters ensured that the ranks of the BEF and Naval Services swelled.

By early 1915, women's role in the war had changed. The expectation of a short conflict was not realised, and as men and boys from all trades and professions enlisted, it was left to women to replace them. Over the next four years the effective work of women in heavy industry, transport, agriculture, engineering, banking, commerce, management and administration would shatter the long-held assumption that, in warfare, women were only useful for fund raising, knitting, nursing and recruiting.

Women made up most of the workforce of the vital munitions industry, coping with arduous and dangerous work. Twelve thousand women and girls worked on the 'devil's porridge' (cordite) at HM Factory Gretna alone; a verse from Susan M. Ferguson's poem 'Bravo! Dornock' reflects their attitude:

> War's a grim and weary task
>   For the lads across the foam,
> Work a-plenty now we ask,
>   Since we're lonely here at home;
> Tommy's watchful in his trench,
>   Where the deadly bullet hums;
> We'll be faithful at the bench,
>   'Perseverance overcomes.' [2]

Public Giving

The Scottish branch of the British Red Cross Society worked independently from the parent body in London and, unlike other UK branches, enjoyed a high degree of autonomy. At the outbreak of the hostilities, the Scottish branch established a war executive committee under the Chairmanship of Sir George T. Beatson. Immediately it set about increasing voluntary staff, establishing suitable stores accommodation, and organising medical and surgical supplies for the front. The goal of the committee was to supply comforts for the troops without wasting money, materials or the efforts of the paid and voluntary personnel. The unspoken rule of the Scottish branch was efficiency, economy and endeavour.

In accordance with the War Office scheme for the organisation of Voluntary Aid in Scotland, there were 459 Scottish

Voluntary Aid Detachments with 15,000 volunteers placed at the disposal of the military authorities. In the opening months of the war, hospital equipment, a fleet of motor ambulances and the first mobile operating theatre were gifted to the War Office by public subscription and under the auspices of the Scottish branch. On the home front, rest rooms for troops were established at Aberdeen, Arbroath, Bonar Bridge, Dingwall, Edinburgh, Glasgow and Larbert railway stations. Additionally, 166 Red Cross auxiliary hospitals were established in Scotland for the duration of the war; these were staffed by volunteers and equipped by public subscription. A report into the activities of the Scottish branch during the war years claimed that 'it was ungrudging personal effort' of the Scottish people that was at the heart of effective humanitarian aid.[3]

Loss and Remembrance

In November 1918, when the silence of the Armistice became a reality, some wondered if it would ever be possible to resume a normal life. Going into the war was easier than coming out of it. For five years the vocabulary of war dominated social and political discourse. The common denominator was grief. The loss of life affected every social class: Herbert Asquith, who had been Prime Minister at the outbreak of the war, lost his son Raymond; Andrew Bonar Law, Canadian-born son of a Scottish clergyman, Scottish MP, and wartime Chancellor of the Exchequer, lost two sons, and Sir Arthur Conan Doyle and Harry Lauder lost beloved members of their families. Death was not selective, and grieving, distraught families, lovers and friends turned to a variety of beliefs and rituals to accommodate their losses.

During the war, street shrines constructed by local communities as an outward demonstration of collective grief became popular in cities, towns and villages. These varied in size, craftsmanship and content. Some were wooden boards or thick wooden or metal plaques, on which the names of the war dead were inscribed, painted or carved. They were erected as a labour of love and were maintained by communal grief. Later they were replaced by official monuments and civic memorials. The location of many Scottish memorials signifies the remoteness of the areas where many of the volunteers and recruits had lived.

It was the land-owning families in the Highlands who encouraged recruitment, not the recruiting sergeant. The notion of clan loyalty and martial tradition did much to swell the ranks of Highland regiments. However, the cost was high and there was a significant reduction in returning and able-bodied men to the Highland and Island communities.[4]

In addition to shrines and memorials, it was not uncommon for mourning families to commission an 'in memoriam' poem to be placed in the newspaper, generally written by the local clergy or a newspaper staff writer.

The tragedy of loss was not confined to the fighting fronts: between 1915 and 1918 there were three military disasters on the home front. On 22 May 1915, the Quintinshill rail disaster occurred near Gretna Green.[5] The crash involved five trains and the estimated death toll was 226 with 246 injured. The dead were primarily Territorial Army soldiers of the 7th (Leith) Battalion of the Royal Scots, who were on their way to Gallipoli. On New Year's Eve 1915, *HMS Natal* was destroyed in the Cromarty Firth by an internal explosion; 360 lives were lost, the death toll including three nurses from the hospital ship *Plassey* who had been invited to attend a New Year reception on the *Natal*.[6]

On New Year's Eve 1918, His Majesty's Yacht *Iolaire* left the Kyle of Lochalsh for the island of Lewis, carrying servicemen from Lewis and Harris who were returning home. In the early hours of the morning, as it approached the port of Stornoway, the ship hit rocks at the Beasts of Holm and eventually sank. The final death toll was officially 205, of whom 181 were islanders. The *Iolaire* tragedy had an enormous effect on the community. It was a cruel irony, met with disbelief and incredulity, that men who had survived the war should be drowned within sight of Stornoway harbour.[7]

Throughout the war years the Scots made a huge contribution and their losses were substantial. The total number of Scottish war-related deaths, including the men and women from the Scottish diaspora who served in Dominion or other Forces, has yet to be established but the most quoted figures range between 85,000 and 150,000. There were 43,000 deaths in the naval services, but there is still no definitive Scottish figure within that total. The Shetland Roll of Honour gives an indication of losses from the island communities from which many of the naval enlistments were drawn: Shetland lost 321 men and boys from the naval services.[8]

Amongst the war statistics, we find that 354 regimental pipers lost their lives, and of the 378 nurses from Britain, Ireland and the Dominion nursing services who died of war-related injury or disease, 40 came from Scotland. Many Scottish nurses were Mentioned in Dispatches or received the Military Medal, some were acknowledged with both. Within the ranks of the Regular and Territorial Forces, Scottish recipients of the Victoria Cross numbered 74.

At the outbreak of the war in August 1914 every Regular Scottish Regiment mobilised for the fighting front: the Royal Scots Dragoon Guards, the Scots Guards, the Royal Scots, the Royal Highland Fusiliers, the Royal Scots Fusiliers, the Highland Light Infantry, the King's Own Scottish Borderers, the Cameronians, the Black Watch, the Seaforth and Cameron Highlanders, the Gordon Highlanders, and the Argyll and Sutherland Highlanders. They were later supported by their many Territorial and Service Battalions.

The Scottish Regiments were deployed in every field of military operations from France and Flanders to Gallipoli, Mesopotamia, Italy, East Africa, Salonika and North Russia (Royal Scots battalions were deployed there and in Georgia until April/June 1919). By the end of the war it was estimated that the number of Scots serving in the Forces was 688,416. This figure represents 71,707 in the Royal Navy, 584,098 in the Army, and 32,611 in the Royal Flying Corps/Royal Air Force. However, the figures are estimates and should not be considered definitive.[9] The numbers of returning sick, wounded, blind, deaf, mute, disfigured and psychologically traumatised have never been calculated. By 1919 and beyond, many mothers, wives, sisters and daughters were unofficial carers of their war-damaged loved ones. There was not a single community in Scotland that was not affected by the deaths and disablement of servicemen.

When one of Scotland's most famous literary sons, John Buchan, lost his brother to the war in 1917, an Army private who was at the burial on Christmas morning sent a poem, 'Peace By Christmas', to Mrs Buchan. Although 'The Tweed sings a song of lament', it closes:

Dear boy, when the long night is over
And Liberty's walls are rebuilt,
Surely April flowers will be fairer
In the fields where your blood was spilt:
And children shall play 'neath the green tree
Rich valleys with gold will dance,
Because you gave for Freedom
Your soul and your dust for France.

NOTES

1. B. G. Morrison, *Desert Sands 'Neath Silver Stars* (1918).

2. Postcard in the Devil's Porridge Museum collection.

3. *Record of War Work: An Appeal 1914–1916*, Scottish Branch, The British Red Cross Society.

4. C. M. M. Macdonald and E. W. McFarland (eds), *Scotland and the Great War* (East Linton: Tuckwell Press, 1999).

5. Lt. Col. E. Druitt, 'Accident at Quintinshill 22 May 1915', Board of Trade Report, June 1915.

6. A. C. Hampshire, *They Called it Accident* (London: William Kimber and Co., 1961).

7. John Macleod, *When I Heard the Bell: The Loss of the Iolaire* (Edinburgh: Birlinn, 2009).

8. *Shetland's Roll of Honour and Roll of Service*, edited by Thomas Manson (Lerwick, 1920).

9. *Scotland's War 1914–1919*, University of Edinburgh, www.scotlands-war.ed.ac.uk.

Green Boughs

My young, dear friends are dead,
All my own generation.
Pity a youthless nation,
Pity the girls unwed,
Whose young lovers are dead.
They came from the gates of birth
To boyhood happy and strong,
To a youth of glorious days,
We give them honour and song,
And theirs, theirs is the praise.
But the old inherit the earth.
They knew what was right and wrong,
They were idealists,
Clean minds, my friends, my friends!
Artists and scientists,
Their lives that should have been long!
But everything lovely ends.
They came from college and school,
They did not falter or tire,
But the old, the stupid had rule
Over that eager nation,
And all my own generation
They have cast into the fire.

Naomi Mitchison

Women Demobilised

July, 1919

Now we must go back again to the world
Full of grey ghosts and voices of men dying,
And in the rain the sounding of Last Posts,
And Lovers' crying –
Back to the old, back to the empty world.

Now are put by the bugles and the drums,
And the worn spurs, and the great swords they carried,
Now are we made most lonely, proudly, theirs,
The men we married:
Under the dome the long roll of the drums.

Now are the Fallen happy and sleep sound,
Now, in the end, to us is come the paying,
These who return will find the love they spend,
But we are praying
Love of our Lovers fallen who sleep sound.

Now in our hearts abides always our war,
Time brings, to us, no day for our forgetting,
Never for us is folded War away,
Dawn or sun setting,
Now in our hearts abides always our war.

May Wedderburn Cannan

Gallipoli

(Anniversary)

Ghosts man the phantom ships that ply between.
White ships with sails of mist and bleaching prows,
Ply through the night, with freight of unkept vows
And haggard men. The waters stretching green
Into the distant bay, roll to the shore
With ominous music, and the dawn creeps slow
On frightened feet across the hills, till lo,
The ghastly prows are turned, and there once more
The boats are lowered and filled, and through the dark
Bewildered waters crouching men cling close
On anxious oars. 'A landing! Now!' Dim rows
Bleeding, insensate, mark the waiting sand,
Heedless they rush, blanched, frenzied, staring, stark,
Dead men, – eternally, they land, they land!

Mary Morison Webster

In a Tramcar

Rain, dark, and mud; the gaslights dim and shrunk;
  Dull full-fed faces ranged in double row,
Oozing respectability; and, drunk,
  Within his corner, mounting in a glow
Of mirth that is not mirth, he sat and sang
  Of Afton's green braes. His friend, mean, shoddy-clad,
And hunched and writhen, in a voice that rang
  Strange on those stolid masks, explained: 'This lad
(I dinna ken him; I'm just seeing him through)
  Got blinded at the war. He's no' himsel'.'
Then suddenly I saw his eyes were two
  Red smears. The conductress signed and rang the bell.
  They lumped him out into the triple night
  Of dark and mental mirk and blasted sight.

Edward Albert

The Street

November 11th

The clash of traffic, and innumerable feet
Shuffling along the wide grey pavement:
A news-boy's cry above the steady bleat
Of gaunt kerb-vendors; and the street
Tapering into the chill November haze.
A sullen roll of gun-fire shakes the air,
Strong as a voice from heaven; children stare
As silence moves down avenues of pray'r.
Sudden, along the desolated street
Burgeons a proud procession: strong, silent feet
Marching from out the dust of far-off days;
Moving to strange thin music as it plays
About their brows. As conquerors they tread
Down the long avenue of shaded eyes,
And on, into the labyrinths of the skies
To mingle laughter with the mighty dead.
Again the sullen knolls of gun-fire creep
Into the silent city; and the air
Rumbles with hum of reawakening traffic –
Slowly across the muddy thoroughfare
An agèd scavenger begins to sweep.

William Soutar

The Soldiers' Cairn

Gie me a hill wi' the heather on't,
    An' a reid sun drappin' doon,
Or the mists o' the mornin' risin' saft
    Wi' the reek owre a wee grey toon.
Gie me a howe by the lang Glen road,   [hollow]
    For it's there 'mang the whin and fern
(D'ye mind on't, Will? Are ye hearin', Dod?)
    That we're biggin' the Soldiers' Cairn.   [building]

Far awa' is the Flanders land
    Wi' fremmit France atween,   [unfamiliar]
But mony a howe o' them baith the day
    Has a hap o' the Gordon green.
It's them we kent that's lyin' there,
    An' it's nae wi' stane or airn   [iron]
But wi' brakin' herts, an' mem'ries sair,
    That we're biggin' the Soldiers' Cairn.

Doon, laich doon the Dullan sings —
    An' I ken o' an aul' sauch tree,   [willow]
Where a wee loon's wahnie's hingin' yet   [lad's fishing rod]
    That's dead in Picardy;
An' ilka win' fae the Conval's broo
    Bends aye the buss o' ern,   [alder bush]
Where aince he futtled a name that noo   [whittled]
    I'll read on the Soldiers' Cairn.

Oh! build it fine and build it fair,
    Till it leaps to the moorland sky —
More, more than death is symbolled there,
    Than tears or triumphs by.
There's the Dream Divine of a starward way
    Our laggard feet would learn —
It's a new earth's corner-stone we'd lay
    As we fashion the Soldiers' Cairn.

....

Lads in your plaidies lyin' still
  In lands we'll never see,
This lanely cairn on a hameland hill
  Is a' that oor love can dee;
An' fine an' braw we'll mak' it a',
  But oh, my Bairn, my Bairn,
It's a cradle's croon that'll aye blaw doon
  To me fae the Soldiers' Cairn.

Mary Symon

Poppies

No great triumphal march
  For lads like you;
No pasteboard victory arch,
  No grand review.
In working raiment brown
  You gave your best;
Then laid you weary down,
  And took your rest.

But the great kindly earth,
  That hid your face,
Gave all your triumph birth
  Beside your resting-place.
The poppy armies blaze
  Red in the holy loam,
And the lark's music plays
  The victors home.

J. B. Salmond

Gin I Was God

Gin I was God, sittin' up there abeen,
Weariet nae doot noo a' my darg was deen,   [work was finished]
Deaved wi' the harps an' hymns oonendin' ringin', [wearied]
Tired o' the flockin' angels hairse wi' singin',
To some clood-edge I'd daunder furth an', feth,
Look ower an' watch hoo things were gyaun aneth.
Syne, gin I saw hoo men I'd made mysel'
Had startit in to pooshan, sheet an' fell,   [poison, shoot and kill]
To reive an' rape, an' fairly mak' a hell
O' my braw birlin' Earth, – a hale week's wark –
I'd cast my coat again, rowe up my sark,   [roll up my shirt]
An', or they'd time to lench a second ark,
Tak' back my word an' sen' anither spate,   [flood]
Droon oot the hale hypothec, dicht the sklate,   [whole show, wipe the slate]
Own my mistak', an', aince I'd cleared the brod,   [board]
Start a'thing ower again, gin I was God.

Charles Murray

BIOGRAPHICAL NOTES

EDWARD ALBERT (1890–1944)
Edward Albert was a popular novelist of the 1920s–30s, writing a series of stories dealing with Scottish life, including *Herrin' Jennie*; and the author of textbooks for senior school English. He was head English master at George Watson's College in Edinburgh at the time of his death, having been on the staff there since 1910. A keen rugby player when young, he was also one of the pioneers of the Youth Hostel movement in Scotland. During the First World War Albert served in the Royal Flying Corps.

DAVID J. BEATTIE (1881–1964)
David Johnstone Beattie was a native of Langholm, and although he spent his adult years in Carlisle he never lost his love for his native town and its history. He is credited with collecting and preserving the history of the town in prose and poetry in his three books, the first being the 1915 collection *Oor Gate-en'*. He was a member of the Plymouth Brethren, a prolific writer of hymns, and the author of two books on hymns and sacred songs.

F. V. BRANFORD (1892–1941)
The son of two English actors, Frederick Victor Branford was brought up in Ardgay, Ross-shire by an aunt, and educated at Tain Academy and Edinburgh University. He served in the Royal Naval Air Service. In March 1917, as a Flight Sub-Lieutenant, flying a Sopwith Pup, he was shot down over the Netherlands and interned. Most of his poetry was written in the period after internment, the war poems published in *Titans and Gods* (1922). Branford was deeply affected by his experiences, and underwent psychiatric treatment, and although great things were expected of him, not least by Hugh MacDiarmid, he ceased writing poetry in the mid-1920s.

JOHN BUCHAN (1875–1940)
John Buchan, who became first Baron Tweedsmuir, combined a literary life with his career in public service. In the latter he rose to become Governor General of Canada; as an author he is best remembered for his popular adventure stories, such as *The Thirty-Nine Steps*. Though not fit for active service, Buchan was commissioned as an officer in the Intelligence Corps in 1916, and in 1917 was appointed Director of the

newly formed Department of Information. He was a joint author of the 24-volume *Nelson's History of the War*. His poetry in Scots outranks that which he wrote in English; his *Poems Scots and English* came out in 1917, and the poems about the First World War have been much anthologised.

MAY WEDDERBURN CANNAN (1893–1973)

As May Cannan's name shows, she was descended from two old Scottish families, and during her youth she spent many weeks in Scotland annually. In 1911 she registered in one of Oxford's Voluntary Aid Detachments, took on the role of quartermaster and set up a hospital ready for the advent of war. In 1915 she volunteered at the Rouen railhead canteen, then in 1918 worked for the Bureau of Central Intelligence in Paris. Through the war and afterwards she worked for Oxford University Press. *In War Time: Poems* was published in 1917; two more collections of poetry followed, and an autobiography, *Grey Ghosts and Voices*, was published posthumously in 1976.

W. D. COCKER (1882–1970)

An employee of Glasgow's *Daily Record* and *Evening News* for over fifty years, W. D. Cocker was a prolific writer, producing plays, short stories and much popular poetry (*Poems Scots and English*, first published in 1932, is still in print); in a more serious vein was the handful of poems he wrote during the First World War. Enlisted in the 9th HLI (the Glasgow Highlanders) in 1914, he was transferred to the Royal Scots in 1915, taken prisoner at the beginning of the Passchendaele offensive and imprisoned at Enger, near Minden; the poetry he wrote there deals with war as a theme, rather than directly with his captivity.

DÒMHNALL RUADH CHORÙNA/
DONALD MacDONALD (1887–1967)

Dòmhnall Ruadh Chorùna served with the Cameron Highlanders in France until wounded during the Battle of the Somme, and later in the war with a Field Regiment. His poems express the horror of the front-line soldier in the face of modern warfare. He is perhaps the best-known of the Gaelic-language poets of the trenches, despite the fact that he did not himself write the poems down – they were transcribed before his death, and published in two editions, the second one bilingual, edited by Fred Macaulay, and published under the title *Dòmhnall Ruadh Chorùna: Orain is Dain* in 1995. He returned to his native Uist after the war, and worked for most of his life as a builder and stone-mason.

JEAN GUTHRIE-SMITH (1895–1949)

Jean Guthrie-Smith was born in Glasgow. Early in life she developed a strong sense of social justice, apparent in the poems she submitted to newspapers and magazines at the time, and was influenced by the women's suffrage movement. She attended the London School of Economics, and became a member of the Labour Party. Her fiancé, a serving soldier, was wounded at the Somme and later survived the flu pandemic; she herself undertook welfare work and war work. Her poems are collected in *Adventure Square* (1922).

IAN HAY (JOHN HAY BEITH) (1876–1952)

Manchester-born John Hay Beith was of Scottish descent, and was both pupil and master at Fettes College. Already a full-time author by 1914, Beith joined the Argyll and Sutherland Highlanders and was in France by April 1915, one of the 'First Hundred Thousand', which epithet he took for the title of the collection of good-humoured articles on life at the front, written by him as 'Junior Sub'. He was awarded an MC for bravery during the Battle of Loos and was promoted to Major and seconded to the British War Mission in the USA. Beith served as Director of Public Relations at the War Office during the first few years of the Second World War.

JOHN HOGBEN (d. 1937)

A native of Edinburgh, Hogben was, at retirement, the Secretary of the Standard Life Assurance Company. He wrote quite widely on liter-ature, and edited three volumes of the Canterbury Poets series. His own output included humorous rhymes on golf, under the pseudonym 'Cleeke Shotte', and *The Highways of Hades: War Verses* (1919). He was a prominent member of Edinburgh's literary societies, and was Captain of Duddingston Golf Club in the 1920s.

WILLIAM HUTCHESON (1883–1951)

William J. Fraser Hutcheson grew up on Clydeside, was apprenticed in the Fairfield shipyard in Govan and studied naval engineering at Glasgow Technical College. In 1914 he joined the 17th Territorial Battalion of the Highland Light Infantry, and saw active service until 1917 when the War Office transferred him to be Assistant Controller of Shipbuilding and Engineering in India. A published poet (largely in Scots) before the war, Hutcheson contributed many verses to *The Outpost*, the battalion newspaper, some of which were included in one of his later collections, *Chota Chants* (1937). Demobbed in 1919, he married, settled in Glasgow, and practised as a civil engineer until retirement.

VIOLET JACOB (1863–1946)

Violet Jacob was born near Montrose, and lived in India and England after marriage to a British army officer, returning to Angus after her husband's death. She wrote fiction and poetry in English, but her best poetry was written in Scots, with a true ear for the dialect of her native country, pre-dating the upsurge of interest in Scots of the Scottish Renaissance with her collections *Songs of Angus* (1915, 1918). Her only son was killed during the Battle of the Somme in 1916.

R. WATSON KERR (1895–1960)

Roderick Watson Kerr was a journalist, poet and publisher. He served as a 2nd Lieutenant in the Royal Tank Corps from 1916, and was awarded the MC for courage in action in 1918. His collection *War Daubs* was published in 1919, and, though he continued to write poetry, his later work was in a more satirical vein. Kerr worked for *The Scotsman* and, for most of his life, the *Liverpool Daily Post*, and in the 1920s was one of the founders of The Porpoise Press, a small but influential Scottish literary publishing venture.

JOSEPH LEE (1876–1949)

Dundee-born Joseph Lee was a poet, journalist, artist and traveller whose poems and sketches gave the world a glimpse of life in the trenches and prison camps of the First World War. Almost forty, and an established journalist in 1914, Lee nevertheless joined up in the Black Watch, later taking a commission in the King's Royal Rifle Corps. He was captured and spent 1918 as a prisoner of war. His two books of war poetry, *Ballads of Battle* and *Work-a-Day Warriors* were published in 1916 and 1917 respectively. He wrote very little poetry after the war, but pursued a successful career in journalism.

W. S. S. LYON (1886–1915)

Walter Scott Stuart Lyon, from a North Berwick family, was one of three brothers killed in the war. Educated at Oxford and Edinburgh universities, he practised as an advocate in Edinburgh. He had obtained a commission in the 9th Royal Scots in 1909, and arrived in Belgium with the battalion in February 1915; he was killed at the beginning of May in heavy bombardment during the 2nd Battle of Ypres. His collection of poetry *Easter at Ypres, 1915, and other poems* was published in 1916.

UILLEAM MacCORMAIG/WILLIAM MacCORMICK (d.1915)

William MacCormick was born at Tor Mor, Mull. He was an Engine Room Artificer on various ships, and was on *HMS Garry* in 1914 when he wrote 'The Royal Navy'. The poem won An Comunn Gáidhealach's poetry prize and appeared in its magazine *An Deò-Grèine*. MacCormick died in an engine-room fire on board *HMS Hannibal* in 1915.

PITTENDRIGH MACGILLIVRAY (1856–1938)

A leading sculptor, James Pittendrigh Macgillivray became a member of the Royal Scottish Academy in 1901, and was appointed King's Sculptor in Ordinary in 1921. With his lively poetry in the Scots of his native north-east, he was an early proponent of the Scottish Literary Renaissance. His poems are collected in *Pro Patria* (1915) and *Bog-myrtle and Peat Reek* (1922).

GEORGE A. C. MACKINLAY (1890–1917)

Born in Hillhead, George Mackinlay graduated from Glasgow University. He was employed for a brief year as an English teacher at Perth Academy before joining the Cameronians (Scottish Rifles) when war broke out, and was killed in France in August 1917. In 1919 his friends and colleagues gathered his work into a small volume, simply entitled *Poems*, as a tribute.

E. A. MACKINTOSH (1893–1917)

Born of a Scottish father and English mother, and brought up in Sussex, Ewart Alan Mackintosh responded deeply to his Highland heritage. He served in the 5th, and later the 4th, Seaforth Highlanders. Courageous action in 1916 won him the Military Cross, and though wounded and sent back to England, he returned to the front, where he was killed in November 1917. His two books of poetry, *A Highland Regiment* (1917) and *War, The Liberator* (1918), express his keenly felt sympathy with the sufferings of his fellow soldiers and the strong sense of duty he felt towards his men.

MURCHADH MacPHÀRLAIN/
MURDO MacFARLANE (1901–1982)

Murdo MacFarlane was born in Melbost in Lewis, and is known as 'Bàrd Mhealboist'. Too young to serve during the First World War, he was deeply affected by witnessing the wreck of the *Iolaire*. He spent some years in Canada but returned to Lewis, and, apart from army service during the Second World War, remained on the island as a crofter. He was a dedicated campaigner for the Gaelic language and composed many songs which were popularised by the Gaelic folk movement of the 1960s and 70s.

HAMISH MANN (1896–1917)

Arthur James 'Hamish' Mann was born in Broughty Ferry and educated in Edinburgh. He joined up in July 1915, was commissioned as a 2nd Lieutenant in the 8th Battalion Black Watch, and drafted to France in August 1916. He took part in the Battle of the Somme, was wounded while leading his platoon during the advance at Arras in April 1917 and died of his wounds. His parents collected his poetry, most of it written in the trenches, and published it as *A Subaltern's Musings* in 1918.

NAOMI MITCHISON (1897–1999)

Naomi Mitchison is best known as a novelist, and for her role as a lifelong social commentator and political activist. During the war both her husband and brother were seriously wounded; she joined a Voluntary Aid Detachment at St Thomas's Hospital in London. Her early poetry was published in *The Laburnum Branch* in 1926.

MURCHADH MOIREACH/MURDO MURRAY (1890–1964)

A Lewis man, Murray completed his education at Aberdeen University and returned to Lewis to teach in 1913. He joined up when war broke out, and by 1915 was in France as a Lieutenant in the 4th Seaforth Highlanders. He kept a war diary, written in both Gaelic and English, which was published, together with his poems and essays, as *Luach na*

Saorsa in 1970. Moireach continued his teaching career after the war, and served as an inspector of schools.

PÀDRUIG MOIREASDAN/PETER MORRISON (1889–1978)

Peter Morrison was born and brought up in Grimsay, North Uist and worked as a crofter-fisherman. He joined the Lovat Scouts in 1914 and served in the Middle East and France, reaching the rank of corporal. 'Òran don Chogadh' / 'A Song to the War' was composed at Suvla Bay in 1915 and published in 1916; a second version, entitled 'Òran a' Chogaidh' was made by the poet in his 80s, recorded by him and by his sons, and published in his book *Thugam agus Bhuam* (1977).

NEIL MUNRO (1864–1930)

Neil Munro's literary fame is based upon his successful novels and his stories – notably the *Para Handy* series with which he delighted the Scottish reading public in the first two decades of the 20th century. A journalist by profession, at the start of the war he returned to news-paper work, and later travelled to the front as a correspondent. The war concentrated his poetic creativity, perhaps inevitably, as his son was killed during the Battle of Loos in 1915. Poems under the title 'Bagpipe Ballads' were published in *Blackwood's Magazine* in 1917, and in them the sad realities of war, as well as its humour, reflect the pipe music themes of the Highland culture Munro knew so well.

CHARLES MURRAY (1864–1941)

Charles Murray was a skilled and popular poet who wrote in the pure Scots of his native Aberdeenshire, despite spending his working life-time as a civil engineer and senior civil servant in South Africa. He served in the 2nd Boer War, and as Director of Works in the South African Defence Force in the First World War. He returned to Scotland upon retirement in 1924. Three volumes of poetry were published between 1900 and 1920 (*Hamewith* remaining in print since), and his poems on the war, written with a clear eye and without sentimentality, give a picture of the effects of the conflict upon ordinary country people.

W. H. OGILVIE (1869–1963)

Will H. Ogilvie achieved great popularity in Scotland and in Australia, where in his youth he worked as a stockman and rough-rider in the outback, and where he is given national status as a balladeer of the bush. His work ranges from hymns of praise to his homeland in the Scottish Borders, and narratives on Borders history and legend, to sporting verse and witty lines contributed to *Punch*. During the war he deployed his great skill with horses in the Army Remount Service.

JOHN PETERSON (1894–1972)

'Jack' Peterson was from Gruting, on Westside of Shetland. He served in the Seaforth Highlanders and wrote under the pen name 'Private Pat'; his collections of war poetry were *Roads and Ditches* (1920) and *Streets and Starlight* (1923). Peterson was wounded twice and the great influence the war had on him continued to feature in his poetry later in life. His talents for photography and writing and his passion for his homeland were combined in portraits of Shetland in verse and photographs.

MAX PHILPOT (d.1923)

'Max Philpot' was a pen name of W. B. Gardner, under which he wrote in various genres, including his collection of poetry *Many Moods* (1917). A native of Dunsyre and the son of a shepherd, as 'Ralph Fleesh', Gardner wrote dog stories, and as an authority on sheepdogs. He was popular as a speaker on social concerns and as a temperance lecturer.

ALEXANDER ROBERTSON (1882–1916)

Alexander Robertson was a native of Edinburgh, a graduate of the University of Edinburgh, and both pupil and master at George Watson's College. A lecturer in history at Sheffield University when war broke out, he joined the York and Lancaster Regiment (the 'Sheffield Pals') as a private. His battalion served in Egypt in 1915, and were on the front line near Albert by June 1916. He was reported missing on the first day of the Somme. All his poetry was written on active service, with *Comrades* published in 1916 and *Last Poems* posthumously.

MARGARET SACKVILLE (1881–1963)

Lady Margaret Sackville was the youngest daughter of the 7th Earl De La Warr and his wife Constance Baillie-Cochrane, daughter of the Scottish peer Baron Lamington. She started writing poetry in childhood, and from 1900 onwards published 21 books, mostly poetry. During the war she took a pacifist stance; her poem 'Nostra Culpa' (*Pageant of War*, 1916) famously denounced women who supported the conflict as betrayers of their men-folk. Lady Margaret spent much of her adult life in Edinburgh, where she was very much a part of the literary life of the city, and was the first President of Scottish PEN.

J. B. SALMOND (1891–1958)

Arbroath-born James Bell Salmond was a journalist in London at the outbreak of war; he was commissioned as a 2nd Lieutenant in the 7th Black Watch in 1915, and was involved in several of the battles of the Somme. In June 1917 he was admitted to Craiglockhart War Hospital, and during his months there edited the hospital magazine, *The Hydra*, with Wilfred Owen. After the war Salmond returned to Scotland and joined the staff of the *Dundee Advertiser*, and later became editor of the *Scots Magazine*. He wrote several books of non-fiction, including a history of the 51st (Highland) Division, and one collection of poetry, *The Old Stalker and Other Verses* (1936).

ROBERT SERVICE (1874–1958)

Robert Service, the son of a Glasgow banker and his English wife, was born in Preston but spent his childhood in Scotland, which he left at the age of twenty-one to seek work and adventure in Canada. The ballad-style poems he wrote during the early 1900s were instantly popular and earned him the title 'the Bard of the Yukon'. In 1913 Service moved to Paris where he married and settled, living in France for most of the rest of his life. Not accepted by the army, he worked as a war correspondent for the Toronto Star, then from 1915 served as an ambulance driver for the American Red Cross. His war poetry was published in *Rhymes of a Red Cross Man* (1916) and *Ballads of a Bohemian* (1921).

CHARLES HAMILTON SORLEY (1895–1915)

Only the first few years of Sorley's brief life were spent in his native Scotland; until late 1913 he lived in Cambridge and was educated at Marlborough. He travelled briefly in Germany until war was declared, then took a commission in the Suffolk regiment, serving in France from May to October 1915, when he was killed during the Battle of Loos. His poetry and letters show remarkable talent and individuality for one who was only just past his teenage years when he died. *Marlborough and Other Poems* was published in 1916.

WILLIAM SOUTAR (1898–1943)

One of the poets of the Scottish Renaissance, Soutar started to write in Scots for both adults and children in the 1920s. While serving in the Navy during the First World War he contracted an illness which led to ossification of the spine, and was confined to bed for the last thirteen years of his life; this did not diminish the humour and power of his poetry. His literary output also included extensive diaries and journals. Some of his poetry was collected in 1948, and new selections made in 1988 and 2001.

J. E. STEWART (1889–1918)
John Ebenezer Stewart was born in Coatbridge, attended the University of Glasgow, and became a teacher at Langloan School, Coatbridge. He was commissioned in the 8th Battalion the Border Regiment, which saw action in France from autumn 1915 onwards. Stewart was awarded the Military Cross in 1917, and was killed at Kemmel Hill in the 4th Battle of Ypres in April 1918. *Grapes of Thorns* was published in 1917.

MARY SYMON (1863–1938)
Mary Symon was an accomplished writer and an expert on the people and customs of her native Banffshire. Her conflicting responses to the war can be traced in her poetry, published in magazines and newspapers of the time, from drum-beating exhortations to elegiac pieces which convey the enduring heartbreak of a nation. The long poem 'The Glen's Muster-Roll' was written in 1915, making it one of the earliest poems to portray the futility of the war. Her poetry is collected in *Deveron Days* (1933).

J. B. SYMONS 'RESTALRIG'
A Leither born and bred, J. B. Symons celebrated his home town in his poetry, bringing out *Poems and Verses* in 1914 and *War Blasts and other poems* in 1915.

A. STODART WALKER (1870–1934)
Archibald Stodart Walker worked as a physician in Edinburgh's Royal Infirmary before becoming Assistant Professor of Physiology at Edinburgh University. In the late 1890s he gave up the practice of medicine for that of literature, wrote several books on literary subjects, and edited the poems and letters of his uncle, John Stuart Blackie. He published two collections of his own poetry, including *Verses of Consolation* in 1915. He served as a major in the Royal Army Medical Corps during the war.

MARY MORISON WEBSTER

Born and educated in Edinburgh, Mary Morison Webster emigrated with her family to South Africa, settling in Johannesburg in 1920. She was an influential literary critic for many years and a novelist and poet; her first collection of poetry, *To-morrow: a book of poems*, was published in London in 1922, and several further collections followed.

ACKNOWLEDGEMENTS

Our thanks are due to the following authors, publishers and estates who have generously given permission to reproduce poems:

May Wedderburn Cannan: 'To a Clerk, Now at the Wars', from *In War Time: poems* (B. H. Blackwell, 1917), 'The Armistice', 'Women Demobilised', and extract from 'For a Girl', from *The Splendid Days: poems* (B. H. Blackwell, 1919), reprinted by permission of Mrs Clara M. Abrahams on behalf of the May Wedderburn Cannan Estate; W. D. Cocker: 'The Sniper' and 'Sonnets in Captivity' (III, IV, V), from *Poems Scots and English* (Brown, Son & Ferguson, 1932), reprinted by permission of Brown, Son & Ferguson; Jean Guthrie-Smith: 'In the Canteen' and 'The Soldier's Wife' from *Adventure Square: poems* (Hodder and Stoughton, 1922), reprinted by permission of Mr Stewart Neal; Violet Jacob: 'The Field by the Lirk o' the Hill' from *More Songs of Angus, and Others* (*Country Life*, 1918), reprinted by permission of Mr Malcolm Hutton; Roderick Watson Kerr: 'A Vignette', 'Home', 'The Corpse' and 'From the Line', from *War Daubs* (John Lane, 1919), reprinted by permission of Mr Neill Kerr; Joseph Lee: 'Soldier, Soldier', 'The Green Grass', 'The Bullet' and 'Summing Up!' from *Ballads of Battle* (John Murray, 1916), and 'German Prisoners' from *Work-a-Day Warriors* (John Murray, 1917), reprinted by permission of the University of Dundee Archive Services; Naomi Mitchison: 'Spring 1918' and 'Green Boughs' from *The Laburnum Branch* (Jonathan Cape, 1926), reprinted by permission of Mrs Lois Godfrey; Pàdruig Moireasdan: 'Òran don Chogadh' from *An Tuil: Anthology of 20th Century Scottish Gaelic Verse*, edited by Ronald I. M. Black (Polygon, 1999), reprinted by permission of Pàdruig Morrison; John Peterson: 'War' and 'R.I.P.' from *Roads and Ditches* (T&J Manson, 1920), reprinted by permission of Mrs Lindsay Campbell and Mr Magnus Peterson; Robert Service: 'A Song of Winter Weather' from *Rhymes of a Red-Cross Man* (T. Fisher Unwin, 1916), reprinted by permission of Mme Anne Longepe.

Every effort has been made to trace copyright holders of the poems published in this book. The editor and publishers apologise if any material has been included without appropriate acknowledgement, and would be glad to receive any information on poets and their estates we have not been able to trace.

I am grateful for generous assistance from Jo MacDonald and Margaret Mary Murray in making Gaelic texts available to us, and to Ian MacDonald for assistance with the Gaelic content. I would especially like to thank Robyn Marsack for her encouragement and editorial support.

LM